How to Get into Medical School

The indispensable guide that no student can afford to ignore

Dr Christopher See

KoganPage

LONDON PHILADELPHIA NEW DEL

Publisher's note

Every possible effort has been made to ensure that the information contained in this book is accurate at the time of going to press, and the publishers and author cannot accept responsibility for any errors or omissions, however caused. No responsibility for loss or damage occasioned to any person acting, or refraining from action, as a result of the material in this publication can be accepted by the editor, the publisher or the author.

First published in Great Britain in 2010 by Kogan Page Limited

120 Pentonville Road
London N1 9JN
United Kingdom
www.koganpage.com

British Library Cataloguing-in-Publication Data

A CIP record for this book is available from the British Library.

ISBN   978 0 7494 6140 9
E-ISBN   978 0 7494 6141 6

Typeset by Graphicraft Limited, Hong Kong
Printed and bound in Great Britain by MPG Books Ltd, Bodmin, Cornwall

Mixed Sources
Product group from well-managed forests and other controlled sources
www.fsc.org Cert no. SA-COC-1565
© 1996 Forest Stewardship Council
FSC

Contents

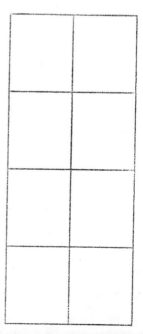

Downloadable template Word documents that appear in the Appendix and free podcasts of mock interviews can be found on the Kogan Page website

To access, go to www.koganpage.com/HowToGetIntoMedicalSchool and enter the password: MED5649

Acknowledgements

I would like to thank all the admissions tutors who took the time to help me understand the real mechanics of the medical school selection process. In particular I would like to thank Dr Roger Carpenter and Dr Don Macdonald from Cambridge University for their help, and staff from Liverpool University and Queen Mary Hospital for sharing their insight on how they undertake selection for medical school. I would also like to thank Dr Robert Tan, my mentor at medical school, without whom none of this would have been possible. I extend a huge thank you to all my students, who are my motivation for teaching and have supported my efforts in this endeavour – in particular Adrianna Liu and Sami Siadati for their help in providing example UCAS forms. Finally, I would like to thank my parents, who have always supported my medical career with compassionate enthusiasm.

Introduction

In the Renaissance, scholars considered themselves to be standing on the shoulders of the great Roman and Greek thinkers of the past. You could consider it a kind of arrogant humility, but they did at least pay homage to the fact that their own excellence came from looking back through history to the examples of others. This book aims to give you some shoulders to at least look at, if not stand upon. There are many stories, good, bad and downright hilarious, but a grain of knowledge or distillate of truth is to be gained from all of them in helping your own application. I bid you to sidestep those mistakes of others and learn from those who have excelled. In my time as a medical school applications tutor, I have met many students and each has their unique spin to add to their application.

A great urban myth is that medical school applications are so difficult because no one really knows what admissions tutors want from you. By interviewing many admissions tutors from a variety of universities, several points have become clear. First, there is a very clear aim of the process, which is to select students who will go on to make good medical students, and eventually good doctors. Second, there is a correlation between successful students and certain attributes seen in examinations, personal statements, references and interviews. Last, this process is not perfect, but the most successful method is to integrate the observation of these attributes and extrapolate what the student will be like as a doctor in the future from what they are like in the present.

Based on this actual process of selection, which is this extrapolation, I have constructed several models to help understand the requirements. These models –

dinner party theory, creativity framework, paper tigers and buyer's remorse – will be explained in due course. Applying them to your application will help you to target the specific requirements that the admissions tutors are looking for. Everyone, including admissions tutors, accepts that the process is flawed, but working towards the real targets gives you the best chance of success.

I find it very easy to stereotype my students on first meeting. However, it is even easier to un-stereotype them as I spend time talking through their motivation for medicine, their interests and their lives. The medical school application is a microcosm of just that. You will first be stereotyped (hopefully) into a potential medical school student by virtue of your paper incarnation. Subsequently, through your personal statement and at interview, you will bring alive your own story and show the admissions tutors that you are a unique and vibrant character. There are some medical school application books which may run the risk of turning applicants into an army of clones. What I wish to do is turn you into an enthralling storyteller. I leave the story of your life and your desire to study medicine in your hands: it is yours to weave as you will. I will guide you as to which threads to bring to the fore and which to leave behind, but your own material forms the fabric and the texture of this story.

One of the keys to becoming a good storyteller is to know your material well. As your life story, your interests and your experiences are the subject matter, I encourage you first and foremost to take a look at your own life. 'What are your passions?' I remember shooting this question point blank at a student during a mock interview session. She froze and didn't have a clue what to say. Only after discussing her interests and passions did I find out that she was a fantastically talented musician, playing the violin from a very young age, but what she really enjoyed was listening to hip-hop music and learning street dancing. A fascinating combination, but more important was the sparkle of genuine enthusiasm that shone through when she was talking about her interests. At that stage, it took some digging from me as the interviewer to uncover this diamond in the rough. There will come a time when you know yourself well enough that the difference between a casual discussion, penning a personal statement and the real interviews will become minimal.

Structure

This book is organized into a flow of processes, beginning with the consideration of medicine as a career and continuing right through until your university place is secured. Chapter 1 gives a thorough accounting of life as a doctor, warts and all. This is designed to ensure that you are fully informed about your choice to study medicine. It also forms a key knowledge base for answering questions about your understanding of the career at interview. Chapter 2 introduces the medical schools and discusses the vast differences between them. Chapter 3 discusses the way in which your academic scores are viewed by admissions tutors, and how they are used to select candidates. Chapter 4 answers the frequently asked questions about work experience and extra-curricular activities. Chapter 5 uses knowledge of the bipolar nature of the medical schools to help design a personal statement specifically for your application.

Chapter 6 discusses the UK Clinical Aptitude Test (UKCAT) and BioMedical Admissions Test (BMAT), providing sample questions and frameworks for answering. Chapter 7 is a comprehensive round-up of information about interviews gleaned from admissions tutors. It details how to recognize patterns and apply interview theory to successfully display the attributes sought by the interview panel. Chapter 8 deals with two special subgroups of applicants, graduates and international students, for whom there are specific challenges to be met and additional methods for achieving an outstanding application. Chapter 9 is a list of further resources to help you pre-pare for all stages of the medical school admissions process.

I hope that you will enjoy all aspects of this process from start to finish. It is a wonderful journey to embark on, and at this stage I am sure you are truly excited by the prospect of a new future and career ahead of you. Use this book as a starting block for pursuing your genuine interest in the medical field. You will find that the theory of storytelling, scientific reasoning and presentation will continue to be useful to you in your everyday life.

CHAPTER 1

Preparing to be a future doctor

How this chapter will help you get into medical school

Committing to study medicine is a decision you make when only 16 or 17 years old, and that will affect the entire course of your life. It is important that you fully understand the course in which this decision will take you, in order to prepare a convincing and successful application.

One of the most common problems I've had in meeting students for the first time is typified by the following short conversation:

Tutor   So, why did you choose medicine?
Student   I've always wanted to be a doctor…

The problem with this response is not just that it sounds remarkably unoriginal. It is that it demonstrates a laziness of thought in considering a very serious choice. There are two possible outcomes from this conversation. The first, and more common, is that while the student has some vague notions about what it means to be a doctor, they do not know enough to go on to explain why they want to study medicine. In order to remedy this problem, the student needs to acquire more information, which starts by considering what being a doctor is really all about. This can be supplemented by further reading and undertaking work experience in order to gain an experiential element.

The second most common occurrence is that the student does have a reasonable understanding of a life in medicine, but uses the reply above as their first to describe their motivation. This is an example of poor storytelling technique, and this is remedied by the techniques discussed in Chapter 7.

Therefore this chapter is designed to give you a solid overview of life as a doctor in case the knowledge element is the problem. It details the good, the bad and the ugly sides of medicine. This should encourage you to consider how best to prepare for the career. It allows you to have a deep discussion about your choice with peers, parents, teachers and eventually interviewers. It will give you a competitive edge over other applicants. Not many candidates have an understanding of the on-call system, or what cardiac arrests are really like. Even fewer will describe the disadvantages of medicine in balanced detail. This chapter has a considerable amount of factual detail; you might consider it a mini textbook on the subject of being a doctor, and you can use it as such.

I fully anticipate that a small percentage of readers will be discouraged from a career in medicine. This is a statistical necessity, as not everyone who is considering medicine will be suited for it, once they know all the facts. I make no apologies for this, and I deem that you have been well served by avoiding making a choice you would regret many years down the line. For the rest, a well-contemplated decision is the beginning of the medical school applications journey.

The journey of becoming a doctor

Training

You will undertake medical training for a minimum of five years, with the potential for a sixth year spent doing an intercalated degree. The differences between the medical schools, and the experiences you will have there, are detailed in Chapter 2. However, common to all are some measure of hard work, many scientific principles to understand, and a substantial amount of memorizing. Also common to all are learning communication skills, ethics and law. Alternative routes include taking an undergraduate degree in another subject, which may or may not be medically related. You can then go on to do a graduate-entry medical course which is four years in length. At the end of medical school, you will undertake final examinations, which are almost universally held to be a stressful and demanding period.

Under the current UK system, once you graduate there is a system of formalized career progression which starts after you qualify as a doctor. It begins with a two-year foundation programme (the two years being known as FY1 and FY2) during which you undertake short rotations in various departments, usually medicine and surgery but also including other specialties, and increasingly accident and emergency and community medicine (GP). After the first year, your provisional registration with the General Medical Council (GMC) is converted into a full registration. Before the end of your second year (FY2), you will be expected to choose a specialty for higher training. After competitive application, you will begin your specialist training (ST), which is usually six years in length. If you are unsure, there are 'core medical' or 'core surgical' training posts, from which you can then go on to sub-specialize. After your specialist training ends, you will progress to a consultant position as this becomes available.

Working lifestyles

The working life of a doctor is highly variable depending on seniority and specialty. At a junior level, work is mainly task orientated, with the house officer ensuring that all the necessities for patient healthcare are being undertaken. These include practical procedures such as taking blood samples, arranging tests for patients, writing referrals for other specialists to assess the patient. The junior doctor would also be the first to assess a patient in case of an unexpected deterioration in the patient's condition. An important role of the junior doctor is knowing when to call for senior assistance. Both FY1 and FY2 doctors have protected teaching time each week. As part of their assessment they will have to maintain a portfolio of learning, reflection, procedures and work-based assessments. This is now performed electronically.

Specialist trainee

In specialist training, doctors take a larger role in the diagnosis and treatment of patients. With increasing seniority, ST doctors may run clinics and undertake procedures specific for their department, such as echocardiography (ultrasound studies of the heart) in cardiology. In surgical specialties, ST doctors become increasingly involved in operations. This position was previously know as 'registrar' (so called because the doctor was entered on the specialist register for training), and you may still hear this term used today.

Consultant

The consultant leads the team and is the key decision maker. They run ward rounds, whereupon they will see all of their patients in turn, with the junior members of the team present to update them on the results of tests and on progress. Many ward rounds also involve teaching of junior doctors and medical students. You may get to accompany a team on a ward round as part of your work experience, and it can be a very valuable learning tool in understanding the roles of doctors at various levels of seniority. Consultants also run clinics where outpatients (patients who are not staying in the hospital) come for assessment and follow-up. Consultants are often involved in clinical research and teaching. Consultant surgeons will be involved in operations for a significant proportion of their week.

General practitioner

The lifestyle of a GP is more settled, with clinics in morning and afternoon, typically working 9.00 am to 5.30 pm. During the lunch period, home visits to patients are common, and there is scope for out-of-hours work, with overnight GP coverage often organized within regions. GP training takes five years at present, after the two founda- tion years, and requires a broad knowledge in many areas of medicine, including paediatrics, psychiatry, obstetrics and gynaecology.

Introduction to the hospital environment

On call

A hospital must still maintain its function in the evening, at weekends and overnight. This means that although most doctors will work a 9 am–5 pm shift, there will be a rota covering out-of-hours work, which is known as the on-call system. This involves a skeleton team of doctors covering acute events and emergencies during this time. The rota will be such that you will only cover this duty every so often, with a number of on-call duties per month. On-call shifts can be very busy, involving seeing and treating patients you are unfamiliar with. It is also an excellent learning opportunity in which you are able to be more directly involved in decision making from a junior level. Doctors will typically be on call for a number of nights in a row, and then allowed a day or two to readjust their internal clock to daylight hours. This relative disruption to your normal routine continues all the way to the end of your specialist training years. This is a consideration that is often overlooked by many applicants, and under- standing this system will help prepare you for the rigours of the career ahead.

Consultants are on call, but usually can remain off-site and be contacted by phone for advice.

Cardiac arrests

Doctors will be trained in life support, starting with basic life support (BLS), moving up through intermediate to advanced life support (ALS). These are put into practice when people have a cardiac arrest on the wards, which is to say when they have no detectable pulse or breathing. 'Cardiac arrest, Ward 9, Bay 3' may be announced through your bleeps. Just as in television dramas, doctors actually run to these patients and initiate treatment as soon as humanly possible. This aims to reduce any injury, particularly to the brain as it is very oxygen sensitive, and even relatively short periods without oxygen can cause irreparable damage. It often involves chest compressions, mask inflations (replacing mouth-to-mouth inflations), and intravenous medications such as adrenaline. It does sound very dramatic and exciting, but the sad fact is the success rate of resuscitation is only around 5 per cent.

Hygiene

Hospital-acquired infections are a serious cause of morbidity and mortality in hospitals today. MRSA (methicillin-resistant *Staphylococcus aureus*) and *Clostridium difficile* are two. Therefore it is a requirement to perform hand hygiene in between seeing different patients. This can involve use of an alcohol gel, which you can squirt onto your hand and that evaporates quickly after cleansing. It may also involve a full washing with anti-microbial soap and hot water if you have been physically examining the patient. This means that you will be cleaning your hands upwards of 20 times per day on average. In the operating theatre, even more attention is given to maintaining a sterile environment, and 'scrubbing up' involves a deep cleaning of the hands and arms to remove any bacteria that would be resident on the skin.

Physical dangers

Many medical procedures require use of sharp instruments on patients, such as injections, cannulation and operations. An intravenous (IV) cannula is a plastic device used to gain entry into the venous system, and can remain in place for some time. It is then used to inject medications into the veins without having to repeatedly pierce the vein. As a junior doctor, you will have to place hundreds of IV cannulae. With each procedure, there are associated risks, the first of which is physical injury if you stab yourself with the needle. More frightening is the so called needle-stick injury, in which you stab yourself with a needle contaminated with a patient's blood. There are several serious blood-borne diseases such as HIV/AIDS and hepatitis C (a virus that attacks the liver) that can be contracted. Hepatitis C has a relatively increased frequency in intravenous drug user patients, and cannot be cured. HIV/AIDS can be treated with anti-retroviral therapy but there is no definite cure. Medical students and doctors currently require hepatitis B vaccinations in order to practice, to prevent their acquiring that disease. Overall this means that even on the most tired of nights when you are working, you must ensure that you practice sharps safety or you can put yourself at serious risk.

Hazardous environments

Working in aid organizations such as Médecins Sans Frontières (MSF) or the International Red Cross can be dangerous, particularly in militarized zones or politically unstable areas. There have been incidences of arrests, abductions and deaths of volunteers in these agencies. Less economically developed countries, such as sub-Saharan Africa or India, may also have greater incidences of HIV, which puts workers at greater risk in cases of needle-stick injury or fluid splashes.

Examinations as a way of life

The more astute of you may have noticed that doctors get the letters MRCP, FRCS, etc after their name. These are the fruit of postgraduate examinations required to progress from junior level to more senior posts, and test both academic knowledge and clinical experience. Each specialty has its own examination that involves core scientific knowledge as well as clinical examinations. Membership of the royal college of your chosen specialty is usually necessary for further progression, and requires membership examinations in multiple parts. Getting used to revision and examinations is a habit you will have to acquire to pursue a career in medicine. But a habit you will need to kick is the 'throwaway knowledge' exam technique, which involves cramming at the last minute and maintaining knowledge just long enough to pass an exam and then forgetting it the next day. To take a radioisotope analogy, what you will need to develop is knowledge with a long cerebral half-life that does not decay easily. The sheer number of exams and the length of the examination period (including medical school (five to six years), foundation years (two years) and specialist training can amount to up to 12 years of examinations. Examinations on the job are different from being at school or university, but considerable dedication is required to undertake the necessary revision to pass, especially after a long day's work.

The advantages and disadvantages of choosing medicine as a career

Advantages

1 Rewarding work
   I should say in no uncertain terms that the work of a doctor is immensely rewarding. It is a pleasure to be involved in the healthcare of others, and you feel that you are making a hands-on and active contribution to society. Although the stories that make news headlines often involve disgruntled patients and lawsuits, the day-to-day reality is that most patients and their families are very grateful to the doctors who look after them.

2 Human interaction

There are many jobs that involve a great deal of human interaction, and medicine is one of them. In almost every discipline there is a positive need to talk to people on a daily basis, which gives variety and interest. This varies from patients to other doctors, as well as other members of the healthcare team.

If you enjoy a hands-on career (as one student described it, 'I'd like to be a human body engineer'), then not only is surgery an attractive option, but even branches of medicine are increasingly having procedure-based activity such as bronchoscopy for respiratory physicians and gastroscopy for gastroenterologists. Both use flexible optical fibre cameras to investigate the lungs or stomach from the inside.

3 Defined career path

The current career path is set out by 'Modernising Medical Careers', a programme for postgraduate medical training introduced in the UK from 2005 onwards, which gives a degree of predictability in how your training will develop. There are also opportunities for gap years and time out of training for pursuits such as research or to pursue personal goals such as sporting or business endeavours.

The financial progression is predictable. The 2009 annual salary figures were around £33,285 for FY1 and £41,285 for FY2 doctors. ST doctors earn between £44,117 and £69,369. Consultants can earn between £74,504 and £176,242.

4 Lifelong learning

Practising medicine requires you to draw on a large body of knowledge on a daily basis. This knowledge base must be kept up to date and accurate, and there are many opportunities in on-the-job training, courses and literature to improve your base of knowledge during your career.

Evidence-based medicine is the practice of using treatments that have been shown to be the most effective in clinical trials. This means that doctors will have to keep up to date with new treatments as well as new studies, in order to give the best patient care. New technology and new procedures are always on the horizon, and a career in medicine will never be monotonous.

Disadvantages

1 Long and difficult training

From the beginning of medical school to becoming a consultant takes a minimum of 13 years of training, many of which are accompanied by examinations. Medical school can be demanding, with a high workload. Life as a junior doctor is constantly busy, and as you progress in seniority the pressure of critical decision making can be stressful.

2 Responsibility

Small clerical or numerical errors, such as prescribing the wrong drugs or doses, can cause serious permanent injury or death to a person under your care. If you are concerned about your ability to be responsible on a day-to-day basis, this is a very serious consideration.

You will be in a position that may expose you to lawsuits and the risk of medical negligence or (rarely) manslaughter. Such incidents may end your career and even land you with a jail sentence, depending on the severity of the incident.

You will also be responsible for your behaviour outside work, and even relatively minor infractions of the law can have serious consequences. You may be summoned to the GMC for a disciplinary hearing.

3 Geographical instability

At present, the selection system for higher training is very competitive, and geographical stability may be difficult. Some doctors have found themselves training in less than familiar locations due to the national allocation scheme. This scheme allows you to rank deaneries in order of preference, and your job is allocated according to score. In essence, it can be difficult for everyone to get training in both the specialty and location of their choice, and you may be forced to compromise on one or the other. Such problems are a long way off from those applying to medical school, but are worth considering when thinking about medicine as a career.

4 Working environment

The dangers of the working environment for doctors have been detailed above and are not inconsiderable. In addition, doctors are exposed daily to bodily fluids: blood, faeces, urine and lung secretions. I was vomited on within three weeks of starting work. If this is the kind of occupational hazard you would rather avoid, there are other careers that you might consider. Perhaps more important, doctors are surrounded by ill patients every working day of their lives. If you have found this an unpleasant or depressing environment during your work experience, do you want to spend the rest of your life working in such conditions? There are some medical specialties that are based more away from patients, such as radiology, where you will spend a lot of time looking at images of patients, such as X-rays, rather than at the patients themselves.

I hope I have pointed out some of the less obvious but still important disadvantages for your consideration. The first reason for doing so is to help you decide whether being a doctor, with everything it entails, is a choice you wish to make. The second reason is because having a balanced and reasoned answer in all parts of the application process is important, and familiarity with the disadvantages forms a key part of that.

Medical specialties

The specialties in medicine can be broadly considered to have two branches: medical specialties, which focus on treatment by medication, and surgical specialties, which focus on treatment by operation.

Cardiology

This is the specialty dealing with conditions affecting the heart, such as myocardial infarction (heart attacks), arrhythmias (abnormal rhythms) and heart failure. It involves the interpretation of the electrocardiogram (ECG), as well as other specialist tests such as coronary angiography, where a radio-opaque dye is injected into the arteries supplying the heart to assess them for blockage.

Its related surgical discipline is cardio-thoracic surgery, which often involves procedures such as heart valve replacement.

Neurology

This specialty focuses on the brain and nervous systems. One of the most common disorders is a stroke, which is caused by an interruption to the blood supply to the brain. It can cause a number of symptoms including weakness and speech impairment, and the effects can be permanent. Other diseases include Parkinson's disease, which primarily affects the elderly and causes slow movements, tremors and rigidity. Alzheimer's and other causes of dementia are also within the remit of neurologists.

Endocrinology

This specialty deals with diseases of hormones. The most common disorder is diabetes, which is to do with abnormalities in insulin physiology. Diabetes has many effects on the body, such as affecting vision (diabetic retinopathy), nerves (diabetic neuropathy) and diabetic ulcers, which typically affect the feet. The treatment of diabetes, with medication or insulin injections, attempts to control blood sugar at a normal level to prevent these complications. Other diseases involve hormones controlling metabolism (such as hyperthyroidism and hypothyroidism) and growth hormones (such as acromegaly).

Gastroenterology

Gastroenterologists tackle diseases affecting the whole length of the digestive system. These include stomach ulcers, which are small bleeding lesions of the stomach wall.

They can be caused by infection with a specific bacterium (*Helicobacter pylori*), as well as long-term use of some medications such as aspirin. Inflammatory diseases such as Crohn's disease and ulcerative colitis are also treated.

Hepatology

This specialty focuses on the liver. One of the major causes of liver disease in the UK is alcohol abuse. In the long term this can causes cirrhosis of the liver, which is a shrinking and damaging of the liver's delicate cellular architecture. It also causes problems such as increased pressure in some areas of the venous system, which can result in bleeding from oesophageal varices, which are engorged veins in the oesophagus. Other liver diseases include genetic disorders such as haemochromatosis or Wilson's disease, and infections such as hepatitis B and C, which are both viral infections.

Psychiatry

A psychiatrist diagnoses and treats a spectrum of mental health disorders, such as depression, anxiety, schizophrenia and personality disorders. Treatments range from medications to 'speaking' therapies such as psychoanalysis and cognitive–behavioural therapy.

Surgical specialties

Orthopaedics

This specialty focuses on the treatment of bones. Orthopaedic surgeons see plenty of trauma cases, and perform treatments such as fixing bones back into place using metal plates and screws. They also perform replacements of joints, such as the hip or knee, in elderly patients with severe arthritis. They must become skilled in interpreting X-rays and other imaging such as MRI scans, for diagnosis and planning treatment.

Urology

A urologist is concerned with the functioning of the urinary tract, and commonly comes into conflict with cancers such as bladder cancers or cancer of the prostate, which is a gland surrounding the urethra in males which produces seminal fluid. It enlarges naturally in old age, and determining whether prostate enlargement is benign or cancerous is an important role of a urologist. This is helped nowadays by the biochemical blood test for PSA (prostate specific antigen), which is markedly raised in prostatic cancer.

Ear, nose and throat

Ear, nose and throat (ENT) surgeons deal with a variety of conditions affecting the head and neck, varying from simple ear-wax syringing to removal of cancers. One of the more interesting tests uses an optical fibre camera and stroboscopic lighting to assess the function of the vocal cords, where you can directly visualize the vibrations causing voice and sound. Operative procedures include removal of tonsils from children.

General practitioner

A GP is the first port of call for most patients in the non-emergency setting. The GP operates in a clinic that takes a number of appointments per day, and patients see the GP one-to-one for an assessment. This may lead to the prescription of medication or referral to a specialist (based in a hospital) if the GP deems this appropriate. Most people will have had some contact with GP services, as they provide immunizations for children and are the preliminary point of contact for pregnant mothers. GP practices provide other important services such as family planning.

As GPs see such a wide variety of cases, they must be well versed in all branches of medicine, including paediatrics (treatment of children), obstetrics (pregnancy) and gynaecology (female urinary and genital tract). They will also need experience in psychiatry, as national figures indicate that up to one in four patients suffers from depression at some point in their life.

The multi-disciplinary team

Understanding the working environment of a doctor is also important in obtaining a realistic perspective on your future career. Doctors form part of a healthcare team that covers all aspects of patient care. Doctors are mostly concerned with diagnosis, investigation and treatment of patients. The other members of the team also carry out vitally important functions, and working together involves an understanding of their roles as well as your own. Knowledge of other members of the multi-disciplinary team also comes up as a question in interview, so it is useful to be aware of the following.

Nurse

Nurses form the backbone of the team. Specialist nurses, such as heart failure nurses and alcohol nurses, deal with patient education. Nurses dispense drugs to patients and perform many procedures, such as insertion of catheters, intravenous cannulae and intramuscular injection. Senior nurses will often be a great source of support for doctors from their experience on the wards.

Physiotherapist

A physiotherapist is concerned with the movement of a patient, and makes assessments to see if a patient can safely navigate their home environment. This is particularly important when discharging a patient home from hospital; not only do we need to have dealt with their disease, but also we must consider how they will go about their daily lives. Patients should ideally be safe on their feet, to reduce risk of falling as well as being able to navigate stairs safely. Physiotherapists can help patients with rehabilitation, exercises and walking aids such as a Zimmer frame.

Occupational therapist

An occupational therapist (OT) is concerned with the activities of daily living, which patients will need to perform at home routinely. These include washing, dressing and cooking. OTs will assess a patient's ability to perform such tasks, and may implement practical measures such as tools to assist patients, or recommend the patient have help at home from care visitors.

Secretary

Medical secretaries play an important organizational role in all branches of medicine. In the GP setting they screen calls to allocate appointments in order of importance. In the hospital setting, they coordinate appointments for their team, including clinics and referrals.

Summary

- Acquiring knowledge about a career in medicine is the first and most important step in the applications process.

- Medical school is the beginning of a long journey, after which you undertake foundation training, then specialist training, leading up to becoming a consultant or GP.

- Advantages include rewarding work, human interaction, lifelong learning and a defined career path.

- Disadvantages include long training, physical risks, geographical instability and a challenging working environment.

- There is no such thing as a 'general' doctor, and knowing a little about each specialty may help you to really understand the day-to-day life of doctors.

- Doctors are part of a multi-disciplinary team involving many other healthcare professionals.

CHAPTER 2

Types of medical school

How this chapter will help you get into medical school

In the previous chapter, you were introduced to real life as a doctor and asked to consider seriously whether or not you feel this lifestyle is for you. This chapter discusses the training you will undergo before you enter that world of work. The training is significantly long, five years at minimum for an undergraduate and possibly longer. It is useful for a prospective student to look ahead to the subjects that will be studied, and most importantly to assess your own level of interest. Will you really enjoy studying the structure of the body at university? Do you really want to know about how drugs work? If the answer is yes, it takes you another step further in your journey towards medical school.

Selecting a medical school is very important, as your experiences will vary immensely depending on where you apply. As will be explained later, the selection criteria for different types of medical school vary considerably, and thus your selection can influence your chances of success, depending on what type of student you are.

This chapter will help you get into medical school by showing you how exciting and interesting the course will be, and helping you make decisions about which medical schools to apply for.

Types of medical school

There are three main types of medical school: problem-based learning (PBL) schools, traditional schools and integrated schools. This divide becomes more significant later on, as we consider their individual selection processes for students and how we can use the differences between them to your advantage. However, at this stage in the book, you are picking the medical schools you wish to apply to, rather than the other way around. Assess the school descriptions and case studies against your own personality and interests, to see which might suit you best. In addition, going to open days, reading prospectuses and talking to current students and peers will help you arrive at an informed choice.

Problem-based learning (PBL) courses

PBL-centric medical schools such as Liverpool and Manchester are now increasing in number. The courses are centred around clinical scenarios given to students, who undertake self-directed learning based around each scenario. These courses offer greater freedom than more formalized taught courses, but on the other hand are dependent on student self-motivation: you get out exactly what you put in. If you are more of an independent learner who does not need external factors for motivation, these courses may suit you. If you need formal teaching, assignments and encouragement to get work done, you may wish to consider a traditional or integrated course.

How it works

Example of a clinical vignette: A 70-year-old lady, who lives alone in a house with an upstairs bedroom, comes to your clinic suffering with knee pain. This is a sharp pain that has been getting worse over the past two months, and is most severe at the end of the day. The lady used to be able to walk 10 blocks to the shops for her groceries but now cannot get further than 50 metres before the pain causes her to stop. She has a past medical history of asthma, and had a hysterectomy 20 years ago. She drinks a glass of wine per day, and does not smoke. Her husband passed away four years ago, and she reports that she has been low in mood since then, with low energy and a poor appetite. She finds she is often waking up early in the morning. Her son lives down the road and helps her with her shopping when he can, but is busy with his own two children.

The student group would read through this scenario and create learning objectives from it. These might be, for example, learning the anatomy of the knee, its neurovascular supply, the common causes of knee pain, treatments such as analgesic medications. Social elements are also important, for example learning about types of walking aids, and the role of the physiotherapist in treatment. The meeting would be attended by a facilitator who is usually a doctor or member of staff from the faculty. They would assist the group in drawing up its learning objectives, but would not play an active role in teaching the academic material. The group would then disperse to read up on their various objectives, and meet again after a fixed period to discuss what they have learned and to teach each other as a group.

Another feature of PBL schools is a focus on communication skills. These are taught by covering the principles of communication, such as body language, active listening, summarizing and checking back to the patient. These skills are then practised on actors who are brought in to play the role of patients. Communication skills sessions are usually group sessions, where other students and a facilitator would give feedback to each student on their performance. This allows the students to gain a realistic perspective on how to interact with patients, in a controlled environment. Actors are trained to simulate a variety of situations including angry, emotional or bereaved patients, to challenge students. PBL schools initiate such training at an early stage in order to prepare students for contact with patients, in a controlled learning environment.

UNIVERSITY OF LIVERPOOL STUDENT EXPERIENCE

'I didn't really know much about the PBL system before I arrived, so I was surprised by how much onus was on us to self-study. I did enjoy the PBL sessions once I got used to them, but I do get annoyed when some others in the group don't take them as seriously. In PBL you really get out what you put in, and it is great to be able to plan out your own week. There are voluntary plenary lectures which you can attend on different topics, so you are not left entirely on your own to learn all of medicine! I liked being able to go on to the wards from year 2, and seeing what I would be doing on the job was a good way of motivating me to study anatomy and physiology. There is still plenty of time for partying, and Liverpool is a great city for that!'

Advantages

- Clinical vignettes are a realistic representation of problems that doctors will encounter in their careers.

- Self-teaching study skills will have a long-term benefit, as medicine is a career of lifelong learning even after graduating from medical school.

- PBL promotes teamwork and presentation skills.

- Most PBL schools provide early exposure to patients and ward experience.

Disadvantages

- It is difficult to self-teach some subjects. Students may benefit from direct teaching on complicated concepts such as, for example, biochemistry.

- If you are not self-motivated or experienced in self-study, the adjustment from school can be difficult.

Traditional courses

Traditional courses can be considered in some ways the opposite of problem-based learning. These courses consist of formalized teaching for the fundamental sciences underpinning medicine, and go into depth in subjects such as pharmacology (study of drug mechanisms), anatomy (the structure of the body) and pathology (the mechanisms of disease). For the first three years, learning is based almost entirely on lectures, practicals and small-group teaching sessions (tutorials or supervisions), with minimal patient contact. After three years, students are introduced to the hospital and under- take their clinical training, coupled with clinical and communication skills. Some students may consider it a disadvantage not to see patients early on, while others may feel better prepared to learn about applied medicine with a solid foundation of knowledge. In practice only Oxford and Cambridge offer such a course in the UK. Another con- sideration for applications to Oxbridge is the considerably higher academic demand for entrants as well as fierce competition, and newly introduced requirements for A* grades at A level at Cambridge.

Advantages

- Solid foundation in the medical sciences that underpin modern practice.

- Small-group (two-to-one) teaching may be ideal for difficult concepts in certain subjects.

- Students are taught experimental design and interpreting data, which are particularly useful for undertaking research.

Disadvantages

- Little patient contact in the first three years.

- Heavy workload and demanding timetable.

- Highly competitive entry.

'The part of the course I enjoy the most is the science, particularly having laboratory exercises in pharmacology and physiology where we would undertake experiments. I liked having a firm base of knowledge under my belt before entering the hospital and meeting patients. There is always a lot to do, but I still manage in the last year to be involved in writing for the "Medic's Revue", a comedy based around medicine. I enjoy the collegiate system. Living in a college environment allows me to interact with people from many other disciplines. Also for sport and music, there are competitive college-level leagues that you can join to keep up a high standard, even if you missed out on making the university team or orchestra. Colleges may provide funding for educational trips abroad, sporting equipment and even the elective! [*See below for explanation of 'elective'.*] I was worried about fitting in here but it certainly isn't too posh or snobbish. People are just as ordinary as me.'

Integrated courses

The majority of medical schools lie on the spectrum between these polar ends. This polarity will play an important role in determining your overall strategy for UCAS personal statement and interview preparation, as will be explained in Chapter 5. Integrated courses combine some form of formal teaching with early clinical experience. There is also an element of PBL learning in most schools. There is a variation in the proportions of these ingredients between each school; For example, some London medical schools such as UCL and Imperial are towards the science side, whereas Queen Mary's leans more towards the PBL end. It is important to read the prospectus for each course carefully, and assess how much taught component vs PBL there will be, as well as when patient contact will begin.

Advantages

- A good balance between the two ends of the spectrum.
- Early patient contact mixed with a solid taught foundation.

Disadvantages

- Less opportunity for in-depth learning and research than traditional courses.
- Less freedom of schedule than PBL-based courses.

QUEEN MARY, UNIVERSITY OF LONDON

'Clinical skills such as cannulation and blood taking were taught at an early stage, and I enjoyed getting my hands on medical equipment and learning how to use it. From the third year, we undertake clinical placement with different firms, and the learning environment is quite different – at the moment my supervisor is a scary surgeon! But I still find time to get involved in netball and relax with friends.'

Subjects studied at medical school

Highlights are things that you may look forward to and find interesting:

Anatomy – This is the study of the structure of the human body. It builds on basic knowledge that students possess from school-level biology, and goes into detail about the connections, neurovascular supply and spacial relationships between structures of the body. This is important in understanding the normal state of the body, so that you can identify when something goes wrong in illness. It is particularly important for surgery. In some schools this is taught by dissection of a cadaver, a real human body preserved in formaldehyde.

Highlights: Understanding the position and importance of structures such as the anterior cruciate ligament of the knee or the metatarsal bone – including the infamous broken one in David Beckham's foot!

Pharmacology – This is the study of the mechanism of actions of drugs. You will learn about the structure and function of drugs, and the receptors that they bind to in the body.

Highlights: How interesting substances such as caffeine and alcohol work. Understanding the basis of common drugs such as paracetamol. Learning how the side effects of drugs come about.

Physiology – This is the study of how the body functions. This involves understanding organs and organ systems, and how they maintain homeostasis in the body.

Highlights: Understanding how the body adapts under the stress of exercise. Learning about how the body adapts to a zero-gravity environment in space.

Biochemistry – This is the study of how the body works at a molecular level. Topics include energy metabolism, genetics and replication.

Highlights: Genetics; what the molecular structure of collagen is. How Sarin poison gas functions.

Pathology – This is the study of what causes diseases. Topics include how the body causes inflammation, how viruses cause disease by entering and eventually rupturing cells, how bacteria acquire resistance to antibiotics.

Highlights: Seeing the direct effects of alcohol and cigarette smoking on organs, and understanding how these processes are mediated.

Ethics and law – This is the study of the system of rules and morality that govern human behaviour. Understanding medical law is important to our practice as doctors. From the pragmatic viewpoint, understanding medical negligence helps us to avoid activities that may result in lawsuits. It is particularly important in procedures that can potentially harm a patient, or ones with serious side effects. If a surgeon were to perform the same acts on someone in the street as he would on a patient, it would be considered assault with a scalpel.

Ethics are also vitally important, and although they may not have such obvious consequences as a jail sentence, the actions of the medical profession as a whole must be seen to be ethical so that patients can continue to put their trust in doctors, and the doctor–patient relationship, which is so vital to treatment, can be preserved.

Clinical specialties are also taught, usually by attachment to the relevant medical department in hospital. For descriptions of these, please see Chapter 1.

If these subjects do not sound like something you would be interested in studying, then this is a significant finding. Are you more interested in mathematical or physics problems? Does business, computer programming or economics appeal to you more? Or are you looking forward to learning about the human body, diseases and how to cure them? Answering these questions will help your own understanding of how motivated you really are to study medicine.

Medical school examinations

A variety of systems are used to test your knowledge and application. Written papers testing scientific and medical knowledge are usually multiple-choice questions. Ethics and law questions tend to be set as short-answer or essay questions. For finals, most universities use an OSCE system – standing for 'objective structured clinical exercises'. These are scenarios where a student is faced with a situation involving a real patient or an actor. They are given a set task to perform, such as to take a medical history, perform a cardiovascular examination, or comfort a bereaved relative. Their performance is assessed on a systematic mark sheet against set standards. The tasks are time constrained, and after a fixed time all the candidates move on to the next station, where another task presents itself. This is a test of knowledge, application and communication skills, and is a good indicator of competency for going on to practise medicine.

Special study modules and the elective

The GMC has released a series of guidelines entitled 'Tomorrow's Doctors', which stipulates that medical school courses should contain 30 per cent special study modules (SSM). These are areas of study that might not be part of the core curriculum but are selected by the student as an area they are interested in. They might take the form of presentations, research projects, a literature review or specialist clinical attachment experience.

The elective is a distinct type of SSM, which is offered at nearly every medical school. It is a substantial period of time, ranging from four to eight weeks, during which students can take a medical attachment abroad. It is a chance to sample how medicine works in different countries, as well as to gain further experience in a specialist field that you are considering for your future career. Exciting opportunities include trauma and orthopaedics in South Africa, general practice in rural India or China, or the latest advances in surgery in the USA. Funding from various agencies is available to help support well-planned electives, although competition for such funds is fierce.

Intercalation

Many universities offer the opportunity to take an extra year of study as part of the medical course in order to earn an additional degree, typically a Bachelor of Science (BSc). During this extra year you focus on a particular subject of interest, engaging in research as well as in-depth learning. Subjects most commonly taken are from the medical school topics listed above, focusing on specific sub-topics such as virology or immunology. There may well be options to take laboratory-based placements leading to research projects.

There are several practical considerations to take into account if you wish to intercalate. If you think you might have an interest in research, it is a good way to explore that route further. The additional degree is helpful when applying for specialist training or foundation posts, which are competitive. Your research might lead you to publication, which again helps in your medical CV for senior posts. On the downside, there is the cost of an extra year at university, on top of what is already a long course. Some students do not enjoy the year spent in research and are eager to recommence their clinical studies at the end.

At Oxbridge, intercalation is mandatory and leads to the award of a BA. The range of options is very wide and can include non-medically related subjects such as engineering, physics or law. There is an option of undertaking an additional three-year intercalation to attain a PhD, which is available for students performing very well in their undergraduate examinations. This is an opportunity to contribute to cutting-edge research, usually in a laboratory-based environment. A PhD will involve new contributions to the body of existing scientific knowledge in specific subject areas, often medical investigations, treatments or the underlying mechanisms of diseases.

Summary

- There are three main types of medical school, which can be thought of as lying along a spectrum from PBL to traditional.

- Your experience of medical school will vary considerably depending on which type you pick.

- It is important to understand what subjects you will be studying at medical school, as they will form the basis of knowledge for your entire career.

- Considering whether or not you might find them interesting may be helpful in deciding whether medicine is really for you.

- The medical school elective is an exciting possibility to travel overseas as part of your course and have hands-on experience in a foreign system, and is common to almost all medical schools.

- Some medical schools offer an intercalated degree, which is a year of in-depth study and research. This can be take for interest, exploring a career in medical research and for a useful additional qualification.

CHAPTER 3

Selection criteria and academic considerations

How this chapter will help you get into medical school

As I stated in the Introduction, the medical admissions process is based on very scientific principles. Admissions tutors are extrapolating what you will be like as a medical student and doctor from the information that they glean about you in your current state. They use experience and previous statistics to determine which attributes correlate best with successful completion of the course. These can be divided into three main categories: academic ability, motivation for medicine, and personal attributes. This chapter deals specifically with the first of these three, which is in some ways also the simplest.

First, it is important to demystify how academic grades are viewed, by looking at the history of the academic system in the UK. The concept of buyer's remorse is based on several discussions I have undertaken with heads of medical schools. It explains some of their more serious concerns and why academic grades are viewed in the way that they are. There are specific points for students regarding GCSE, AS level and A level. UKCAT (UK Clinical Aptitude Test) and BMAT (BioMedical Admissions Test) are dealt with in Chapter 6, with example questions and examination techniques.

Finally, this chapter also provides answers that you may find useful to questions commonly asked by students and which seem to be repeated every year.

Selection hierarchy for academic indicators

How admissions tutors view academic grades

To understand how admissions tutors view academic grades, we must understand the historical selection criteria. Before the advent of the AS/A2 system, admissions tutors had to rely on school predictions of A-level results to assess a student's performance at higher-level academics. This led to the use of GCSEs as a baseline indicator, with A-level predictions being treated with a degree of caution. This was because there was a weak correlation between being predicted high grades and doing well academically. GCSEs also represent a different measure of talent, particularly in breadth of ability.

When the A2 system was introduced, AS-level grades were available at the time of assessment. However, medical schools found that there were 'too many' A grades, and thus although having good AS-level grades had a moderate correlation with performance, it was not good at differentiating between candidates. This was a problem because there has always been an excess of applicants to places, and therefore differentiating students was as important as establishing a baseline. This led to the interpretation of having good AS levels as a 'necessary but not sufficient' characteristic for selection. The final step in the evolution has been the availability to admissions tutors of module marks for each AS paper. This allowed them to differentiate more successfully between good students, such that they could select, and thus good AS-level module marks became more highly correlated with successful completion of the course.

The advent of medical school admissions examinations added another dimension to these statistics. One problem was that independent-school students performed better on average than state-school students, when it came to GCSE- and AS-level results. Thus a test that was more impartial, and was a test of aptitude as opposed to how well a student had been taught, was sought. There are currently two specialist medical school admissions tests, the UKCAT and the BMAT. These are specifically detailed in Chapter 6, but are used by some medical schools as part of their academic assessment.

Based on these findings, admissions tutors take an integrated approach to assessing academic ability, with the best correlates of performance used. They currently base their estimation of academic ability on the following criteria, in descending order of importance:

- BMAT performance;

- AS-level module marks (or AS-level grades);

- UKCAT;

- GCSE results;

- A-level predictions.

The reason why A-level predictions rank so low is because AS-level module marks already integrate a great deal of the information about how a student is likely to perform at A level.

The BMAT examination, if it is used, is considered the best correlate with good performance at medical school. However, there is a stronger correlation with a poor BMAT performance and poor performance at medical school. This means that a low BMAT score is a good negative predictor of performance, and low scores will be actively selected against.

However, since only Oxford, Cambridge and UCL currently use the BMAT results, this may not be applicable to you. UKCAT is used by many more institutions, but still not all medical schools. The use of the UKCAT score is variable and may be a cut-off point for a minimum. Most commonly the score is integrated with other academic indicators to determine whether or not a candidate should be called for interview.

Year on year, there is a strong correlation between good academic performance as judged by the applications process and good performance at medical school. In other words, all things being equal, if an admissions tutor consistently picks better academic performers, they will do better at medical school.

Buyer's remorse

The importance of scoring well on the above academic criteria was underlined by the following interview with an admissions tutor.

When I was talking to the head of admissions for a medical school, one topic that came up was the concept of buyer's remorse. This is the concept of a person who makes a purchase but later on regrets what they have bought. In terms of medical school, this is an admissions tutor who accepts a student but later the student goes on to perform poorly, fail or struggle in some way. The tutor regrets his 'purchase' of this student.

The tutor to whom I spoke went on to explain that one of the reasons behind buyer's remorse is that the admissions process is good at testing for certain characteristics such as academic ability and generic communication skills. However, it is poor at identifying motivation for medicine. He described how it is possible to fake this motivation, and that it is common for there to be reasons other than a pure desire to study medicine that push students into choosing this career path. Parental pressure may be one of the main factors, as well as cultural influences, school and peer pressure. He explained that on speaking to these students and finding out the problems they face, it is not a lack of academic ability that causes the problem; in fact, the students are often quite bright. The real problem is the lack of genuine motivation. Students who did not really want to study medicine have a long and difficult course of study followed by a responsible and challenging career, which can be very daunting. Poor results and failure can be a result of the student feeling that they are not on the right course.

This is a problem for tutors, as this poor performance can take several years to manifest, and is a waste as another student could have benefited more from the poor student's place. It is a problem to you as a student because admissions tutors are aware of this and are taking measures to reduce buyer's remorse by looking for evidence of bona fide interest in medicine. With this in mind, aspects of the personal statement and interview advice will be geared towards avoiding the triggers for potential buyer's remorse on the part of the interviewers.

Buyer's remorse is a very real concern for admissions tutors, as it has a serious impact on the lives of the students. It seems as though the main difficulty for admissions tutors is motivation for medicine. We will discuss how to avoid triggering potential buyer's remorse signals in later chapters. However, the other important point is that admissions tutors acknowledge that their selection for academic ability is good. In other words, that is the part of the selection process which functions most reliably. It is therefore easier for selectors to differentiate between candidates on a consistent basis on academic ability.

This is what motivates selectors to look carefully at the numbers in an application. Therefore you will want to score as highly as possible in this area as it has the most predictable increase in your chances of being accepted to medical school. Note that this is different from saying it is the most important factor for medical school selection. Motivation for medicine and personal attributes are equally important, but if you are approximately equal on these two selection criteria, it is easier to differentiate between a high and a medium academic score than between two individuals' reflections on similar work experiences.

GCSE subjects

It is recommended that you undertake separate science GCSEs, as you will go on to do chemistry and/or biology at A level.

There is a minimum requirement of five A or B grades, but as we have discussed above, application for medicine is becoming so competitive that minimums are only a very rough guide. In order to be competitive, particularly for medical schools higher up the league tables, you will need to score a good proportion of A and A*, complementing a broad range of subjects and as many as you can.

Exceptional performance at GCSE is different from exceptional performance at AS level, as the breadth of subjects tested is much wider. However, you should not be discouraged from an application for medicine just because of mediocre GCSE results, and you can partially compensate for this by excellent AS-level results.

For Oxbridge, if you go on to do all science A levels, your GCSEs in history, geography or English may be the only indicators of your essay-writing ability aside from the one sample they get at BMAT.

AS level

AS-module marks are now one of the best indicators of future academic performance, along with medical school admissions tests. Therefore the AS year is the most important year in which to work hard and gain as many marks as possible. More universities are starting to use these results to judge students, and they are particularly important for Oxbridge applications.

However, at the current time AS grades, rather than module marks, are still the most commonly used result, and needless to say it is important to score well in them. There is a minimum requirement of AAB at A level, and if you score below this at AS level, then by extrapolation it is less likely that you will go on to achieve these grades than a candidate who achieves AAAA.

Also, the AS-level year is usually the time when students push on to undertake extra-curricular activities and work experience, and showing that you are able to achieve top AS-level grades while maintaining a wide range of activities and commitments reflects well on you as a candidate. Taking additional AS levels will also reflect this ability to multi-task.

A level

A-level predictions are still used by schools, but their worth has become diminished by the availability of AS-level grades. Therefore they are generally only significant if there is a disparity between the two. For example, for the student who perhaps underperformed at AS level but has an AAA prediction and a strong school reference, their poor performance may be somewhat mitigated. On the other hand, a student with solid AS-level grades but a poorer A-level prediction might be at a disadvantage as the school is imparting their opinion on the student's working ability or attitude as well as projected academic achievement.

A* grade at A level

A* grade is a new grade at A level introduced for the first time for 2010 results. In order to achieve an A* grade, you must achieve an average mark of at least 80 per cent in AS and A2 level, and also achieve an average of over 90 per cent in just your A2 module marks. This is a significantly difficult challenge, and requires consistent and diligent work from the student in order to achieve it.

The A* may impact you in several ways. First, Cambridge is the only university at the time of writing to make A*AA their standard offer for medicine. Therefore, if you think you will be unable to achieve at least one A* grade, you should consider alternative medical schools. Also, if you are not predicted any A* grades, the admissions tutors might think it is less likely that you will achieve the offer.

Second, it means that students taking gap years will have the possibility of attaining A* grades at A level. This is a good way of distinguishing yourself from other students, and is a very firm indicator of future performance – this is because it almost amounts to a module mark score, with the requirement being 90 per cent or above at A level.

Frequently asked questions

'Why do we have to study chemistry for medical school?'

It is often said that chemistry A level is a requirement for medical school entry because it is 'hard'. This has a grain of truth, but in fact the content and principles of the taught matter have some significant practical manifestation in the course. Understanding medical conditions such as metabolic acidosis requires a background in acid-base equilibrium dynamics. The interactions and types of bonds between various side-groups of compounds will give rise to tertiary structures of proteins, for example in collagen. You will also be taught pharmacology, which describes how drugs interact with the human body. Key body substrates such as hydrocarbons and alcohols are also covered in medical school.

'Would carrying on biology for A level this year look better for my UCAS form?'

Some universities do not require biology A level in order to apply for medicine. However, I absolutely recommend that all candidates take biology A level, as the study of medicine is essentially about biology. The fundamentals of anatomy, physiology and cellular biology are covered in the syllabus. The study of medicine could be described as understanding what goes on in the human body when it is functioning normally, what causes it to function abnormally and how to fix those problems. I would be concerned if a candidate proclaimed that they were fascinated by science and the human body but failed to study biology at AS or A2 level. This would give an incongruent impression to selectors, and would be difficult to justify at interview. It would also make it harder for the student once they started the course at medical school, as the basis of many topics at medical school is biology or chemistry. For these reasons, biology A level should be a must for all medical school applicants, regardless of the university's stated requirements.

'What should I pick as my third subject?'

This question is more difficult, and very much depends on each individual candidate. It is best to pick a subject you are good at and are interested in. This could be mathematics or physics, which would complete a scientific academic profile. A language, history or English would give a greater breadth and might make you stand out as a rounded individual when compared with other candidates. There are certain subjects that are seen as 'softer' options and may count against you in the application, such as general studies, media studies, business studies, art, or design and technology. These should generally be avoided as a third subject, but are fine as a fourth and in fact may be an interesting divergence from the norm.

'Should I take a fourth A level?'

This is an exercise in risk management. I would generally encourage students to take the attitude of doing more than the minimum requirements, motivated by their own interest. However, bear in mind that the medical school applications process places a considerable extra burden on your shoulders from the first draft of the personal statement up until the interviews are over. Also, fourth A-level marks are not included as part of the offer. If you feel you would be able to cope with the demands of these, and that your AS marks warrant it, I would positively encourage students to undertake a fourth A level. If you feel you might better spend your time preparing for medical school applications and interview, and focusing on three subjects, that is also perfectly acceptable. It is important that you judge the risks and rewards of taking the extra burden of work before coming to your own informed decision.

Gap year

Both students and parents ask about the advisability of taking a gap year. There are two types of gap year, which are slightly different but both valuable in their own way.

Enforced gap year

This is typically taken when a student fails to gain admission to either their preferred university for medicine, or any course at all. Students will often wish to re-apply, and spend the year undertaking various work experiences and applying via UCAS in the autumn.

Advantages

- Students can often be disheartened and nervous about taking this approach, but there are several advantages to be considered. One of the key points is that the admissions process involves tutors extrapolating a student's academic ability, determination and communication skills many years into the future to estimate if they would be a good medical student and eventually a good doctor. In terms of academic ability, the A-level results with module marks are considered a good indicator of future performance at medical school. However, you have to score well in them to benefit from this, and if you perform poorly it will be strongly negative for your application.

- In terms of dedication, admissions tutors have said that it does demonstrate a commitment to the career choice when a student re-applies after not being accepted anywhere in a previous year. However, this is balanced against the fact that usually candidates are not accepted for good reasons. The message seems to be that admissions tutors appreciate that such reasons can change over time, and a student who has learned from them will have actively demonstrated determination to study medicine.

Disadvantages

- On the negative side, the first consideration is time. The medical course is a minimum of five years at undergraduate level, with the possibility of an extra year of intercalation. Therefore an additional year can make the beginning of your working life seem a very long way away. Cost is often seen as a major obstacle but in actuality this is often mitigated by students working for the early part of the gap year to fund the latter part. This has the additional bonus of giving you exposure to the working environment, and teaching you about the importance of responsibility to your employer and customers. Other considerations include risk of harm if going to dangerous locations.

Unenforced gap year

This is when a student decides to apply for a deferred entry or applies during the following year, in order to undertake a year of activities for their own personal interest and development. Admissions tutors recognize the benefits of increased maturity and world experience that these candidates acquire, and these are generally considered beneficial. Interestingly, you do not have to take part in any medical activities to gain this benefit, as admissions tutors consider this as mostly improving the 'personal attribute' aspect of selection. Activities such as travelling, volunteering and teaching are seen as valuable and worthwhile. Important aspects are good forward planning and being prepared to discuss your intentions with enthusiasm and accuracy.

Advantages

- Increased maturity is seen as beneficial by admissions tutors.

- A-level results with module marks are a more reliable indicator of future performance than AS levels.

Disadvantages

- Students tend to have a poorer performance in the first year.

- Additional time and cost in an already long course.

Summary

- Academic ability is one of three major criteria you are being judged against.

- Admissions tutors recognize that this is the most reliable of the three criteria.

- Having a strong academic base is a necessary but not sufficient prerequisite for successful competition against other candidates.

- Scoring highly in AS-level modules is the most efficient way of increasing your academic ranking.

- GCSE marks are a useful indicator of breadth of academic ability.

- Mediocre marks at GCSE should not put you off applying to medicine, as long as you are prepared to work hard at AS level.

- UKCAT and BMAT scores are also considered highly. See Chapter 6 for how to improve your performance in these examinations.

- Both unenforced and enforced gap years are considered beneficial by admissions tutors, provided that good A-level marks are achieved.

CHAPTER 4

Extra-curricular activities and work experience

How this chapter will help you get into medical school

In the previous chapter we dealt with the academic aspect of the selection criteria. How then shall we demonstrate the remaining two aspects, personal attributes and motivation for medicine?

The most objective way is to build up a portfolio of activities that you can refer to, in order to convince admissions tutors that you do in fact meet these requirements. This chapter details approaches you can take to increase your knowledge and experience of medicine, in order to demonstrate your motivation. It tackles the subject of work experience and the frequently asked questions surrounding it. It also has a section on helping to plan your extra-curricular activities to help your application, while avoiding falling into the trap of making 'paper tigers'.

Motivation for medicine

Let's look at some activities to enhance your understanding of medicine as a career and a subject.

Reading this book is a good start for increasing your knowledge of medicine as both a career and as an academic discipline. Chapter 1 contains details of life as a doctor, the uncut version. If you are still enthusiastic about medicine after that, we are on the right track. Chapter 2 discusses academic disciplines to be studied at medical school, and again if these have sparked your curiosity, this is a positive step. Here are some suggested activities that may go further in developing your interest and motivation:

Reading – Scientific literature, popular science books and current affairs can stimulate your interest in medicine and keep that interest up to date.

Talking to doctors – This can give you a clear picture of what they do and do not enjoy about the job, as well as giving you some insight into the training process.

Scientific endeavours – These can include laboratory placements or after-school clubs, or even your own experiments at home – with due caution.

Work experience – This is detailed below.

Voluntary work – This shares many principles with work experience and can involve anything from volunteering at a charity shop to teaching children, assisting in nursing or residential homes, reading to the visually impaired or any other similarly worthwhile activity. Details are described below under 'Extra-curricular activities'.

Work experience

Most applicants to medical school will have some degree of work experience behind them. This is because it is critical to have a least a working knowledge and some hands-on experience of what it is like to be a doctor, in order to make an informed choice to study medicine. These activities will often involve work-shadowing a doctor in their daily activities in a hospital, GP practice or laboratory. You will probably not be allowed to undertake any direct treatment activities, such as administering any medications or writing the medical notes. This is for patient safety and the rules should be obeyed strictly.

What many students tend to think is that in order to stand out, you must accumulate more than the next person. As a result, many students have a collection of relatively short work-experience placements that they have managed to fit into various holidays in the run-up to application. Below are some tips to maximize the benefit from work experience and to help plan your applications.

Tips

1 Acquire a balanced programme of work experience – one surgical attachment, one medical attachment, one GP placement and perhaps a laboratory or research placement. This will demonstrate that you understand the varied nature of the medical career, and ensures that your exposure will not be too one-sided.

2 Talk to people! Everyone will have a different opinion on the working life of a doctor. Make sure you talk to patients as often as you can. This makes up the bulk of a doctor's work and it is helpful to see how you cope with and enjoy being in that situation. There is also often a great deal you can learn from experienced patients.

3 Keep a diary of your experiences of each placement. In particular, take note of less 'technical' things such as patients you particularly remember. (Make sure these are made anonymous, eg Mr X with a fractured tibia and fibula, who had a hard time coping because his wife was ill at home and he wanted to get well as soon as possible to look after her again.)

4 Use this diary to reflect on what you learned each day. Think about the following questions when you are reflecting:

   – How did you like the working environment?
   – Did you think the doctors were good, medium or bad, and why?
   – What evidence of teamwork, communication skills and empathy did you see demonstrated?
   – How were these demonstrated?
   – What part of the placement makes you most want to go into medicine?
   – Which parts put you off?
   – What were the roles of other members of staff who were not doctors?
   – How would you feel about being a patient on that ward?

Apart from the insight you will gain into the world of medicine, you will use your work experience at two junctures: in the UCAS personal statement and at interview. It is therefore vital that you have this completed diary as a resource to draw upon at those times. In particular, it will avoid your falling into the trap demonstrated by the case study below, of not focusing on the experience element of the placement. I recommend that candidates take a short time at the end of each day of work experience to sit down and reflect on what they learned and experienced that day. It may only be for a short time, just to think and jot down a few notes, but because important and useful memories and thoughts may be lost, this technique will maximize the value of each work-experience placement.

At a mock interview one candidate responded to the question, 'Tell me about your work experience' in the following manner.

'I did a two-week placement at Lewisham Hospital, then three weeks in a residential home, another two weeks in a plastic surgery unit in Paris.'

He then proceeded to cross his hands and flourish a self-satisfied grin.

He was then asked 'So what did you do on these placements?'

He replied 'I went to five operations, followed nurses, doctors and radiologists around, and also talked to patients.'

At no point during his replies did he give any indication about anything specific that he had done or any memorable events. He failed to impress the interviewers with what he had learned or gained from such placements. Most important, his answer was uninteresting and bland, and in order to glean more the interviewer would have had to ask yet another question to 'mine' the information from him. This extra work will not be appreciated by interviewers. The candidate was later rejected from his top choices at UCL and Oxford after receiving interviews. Despite having a strong paper application and a wide array of medical placements, he did not make the best use of them by digesting the experiences he had and reflecting on what he had learned and gained from his time on the wards.

If this candidate had had a rich diary of events and reflections from his work experience, he would have been in a much better position to give a more substantial answer. That in turn would have better demonstrated his motivation for medicine, which is one of the main aims of undertaking work experience.

Another element of this is poor interview technique, and the remedies for this are discussed in Chapter 7.

'Will taking laboratory-based placements help my medical school application?'

Absolutely. First, as we have previously discussed, science underpins medicine and if you have the enthusiasm and get the opportunity to see how laboratory science is applied, then you will certainly gain something from the experience. More important, most candidates have an interest in science, and when they are exploring career possibilities it is not sensible to have based your conclusions on a single type of placement or activity. If one of your main reasons for applying to study medicine is a passion for science, you should have an idea of by what other avenues this could be explored, in terms of both degree-level education and careers. Having a good laboratory experience might change your mind or make you more resolute that you would like to practise science in a more applied and interpersonal manner. Don't forget to reflect on what you thought of the placement yourself, and if you are asked about it let the interviewers know what these reflections were, be they good or bad.

Extra-curricular activities

The personal attributes of teamwork, communication skills, leadership, dedication and empathy are best demonstrated by discussion of extra-curricular activities. The selection of which activities to undertake is a perpetual question on the lips of students. I will address this first with a cautionary tale, and then detail the principles you can use for selecting extra-curricular activities.

Paper tigers

In Chinese tradition, a 'paper tiger' describes a person, object or entity that appears fearsome on the outside but is made of little substance, and therefore under further scrutiny is much weaker or worth less than it first appears. One problem is that when applicants or parents hear that medical schools are looking for a breadth of interest, the hunt of 'things that will look good on the CV' begins in earnest.

A student once asked me 'I've got some good points for sports, music and drama, so what other extra-curricular activity should I do now to improve my application?'

When questioned further, this young gentleman had played a few games in the school's second-team rugby, played the guitar only with friends at parties and had a small supporting role in a school play two years previously. He could not talk in depth or, more important, with passion about any one of his 'good points' that he had on his CV.

In essence, his claimed activities were merely paper tigers, as they sounded impressive on a UCAS form: 'I represented the school in rugby, acted in a school play and enjoy playing the guitar in small-group environments.' On further examination, however, they were not substantial, nor did he have any genuine interest in them.

There are several dangers in taking this approach to extra-curricular activities. The first is that interviewers will be able to assess who has a keen interest in an activity and who is doing it just for show. This is because they undertake interviews every year with candidates who have 'padded' their personal statements – claiming more than they can justifiably discuss at interview. You may also come across a member of the interview panel who has a particular interest in your claimed pastime. It will be a painful experience not to be able to discuss your claimed activity with someone who genuinely knows a lot about, for example, rugby or acting.

I make a point of actively discouraging students from investing in paper tigers, things in which you have no interest but think will look good; it will not benefit you. Even if you do make it into the medical school of your choice, you will have wasted a lot of your youth on things that you do not care about. To look at it another way, there are far too many interesting things to do rather than wasting your time doing something which you have no interest in. If you don't make it in, all the worse, for you have not managed to explore your potential. Worst of all, by just focusing your entire lifestyle on the medical school application process, you may end up coming across as narrow in interest and intellect.

Not everyone is a rugby-playing violinist-cum-actor, nor are all such people accepted into medical school. It is important to have some interests, not for applications but for life, and whatever your interest is, learn to love it and follow it with a passion.

How to choose extra-curricular activities for medical school applications

Principles

Let your interests guide you. Try to tie in your own interests with the activities you are undertaking. If you are a musician but hate reading novels, rather than going to the 'Reading to the elderly' programme simply because everyone else is doing it, why not try to organize a recital or concert to raise money for a charity that you would like to support? Not only will this demonstrate your leadership and innovation, but also you will most likely actually enjoy the whole process, and will do a far better job of it. Having said that, any budding stage actors might love the chance to work on their dramatic range by reading for the partially sighted.

Quality is better than quantity

There is a human limit to how much one can achieve in multiple disciplines. It is relatively rare to find an Olympic-level athlete who also played in an orchestra and undertakes scientific research. It is important therefore that you take this into consideration when selecting your extra-curricular activities. You may wish to explore your limits in a sporting activity, which is admirable, and it is better to focus on enjoying and achieving in this discipline rather than trying to fit in too many other activities for the sake of roundedness.

Objective achievements

It can be useful for the purposes of the UCAS form to have objective qualifications that can express some achievement in a pursuit in a small number of words. For example, 'I enjoy playing the piano' could be said by almost anyone, but 'I achieved Grade 8 in piano' is a very different package. First, it is an objective measurement that has a minimum requirement of achievement and dedication. This is important for giving a solid impression in your personal statement. If the statement is full of 'softer' claims such as 'I like golf, I enjoy playing the piano, and I like running', it is less convincing than 'I achieved a black belt in Shotokan karate, and later pursued my interest in fencing, where I won gold at the London Games 2008 at the under-16 level.' This principle applies for certificates, awards, school colours and top sports team representation.

However, 'not everything that can be counted counts, and not everything that counts can be counted', according to Einstein, and it is important not to become obsessed with certificate counting.

Ensure that your interests are not all 'solo' type

In order to demonstrate teamwork, communication skills and leadership, it is a pre-requisite to have other people involved in the activity. Hobbies such as oil painting, playing computer games, reading and writing poetry, and long hikes through the countryside are wonderful, but if you do all of these on your own, then it will make things difficult for your application. It is important to have at least one group- or team-based activity where you can learn about these attributes, as well as demonstrate them. If you are not very inclined to group work and teamwork, it may be a sign that medicine is not for you.

Voluntary work

You can apply many of the principles of work experience to the completion of volun-tary work. Empathy is one of the key characteristics you should be trying to learn and consider on your voluntary work placements, and that will mainly stem from your interactions with people. Make a diary of your reflections and the people whom you helped through your volunteering, as this will help your own understanding of com-passion, and be a useful resource for UCAS personal statements and interview.

Try not to be influenced too heavily by others

There are many sources of pressure from peers, parents, teachers and others, to conform to a certain mould of extra-curricular activities. As I stated in the Introduction, some of my most talented students have very unusual extra-curricular activity com-binations such as street dancing and violin playing, or basketball and Persian tradi-tional painting. They have gone on to do well at interview, and this is partly because of their genuine interest in things – including hobbies, medicine and science. I hope that you will also follow in their footsteps and take your interests to a high level, what-ever they might be.

Summary

- Motivation for medicine can be demonstrated well through work experience.

- Try to obtain a rounded range of work-experience placements.

- The work-experience diary is a vital tool for the later stages of application.

- Make a habit of reflecting and making an entry into the diary on each work-experience day.

- Extra-curricular activities can be used to demonstrate personal attributes.

- Avoiding paper tigers is a key step in constructing a solid and genuine medical school application.

- In selecting activities, be guided by your interests and try to avoid being influenced by pressure from others to conform.

- Objective measurements of achievement can be useful and should be sought where appropriate.

CHAPTER 5

The UCAS form

How this chapter will help you get into medical school

The majority of the UCAS form is a simple exercise in administration, but the section that is the subject of much fear and speculation is the personal statement. This is the section, along with your grades and reference, that determines your call to interview.

This chapter will detail exactly what it is that medical schools are looking for from the personal statement. Interviews with many admissions tutors reveal that this varies immensely depending on which type of medical school you are applying to, and understanding this is one of the most important steps of getting into medical school.

The bipolar nature of medical schools

It is important to consider how the personal statement is viewed by admissions tutors, in order to understand how and what you must write to succeed. After speaking to several members of staff at medical schools, the main message is that the personal statement is a means of communicating the key attributes. One of the processes of medical school admissions is extrapolating how a school-age student would go on to perform in their studies and eventually in their duties as a doctor. They consider the personal statement a vehicle by which you can demonstrate your current achievements and what you have learned from them, as a basis for making that extrapolation.

The next question is, what attributes are they looking for? One of the most interesting discoveries I made in doing research and consulting with tutors is that the attributes they wish to see demonstrated vary widely depending on which type of medical school you are applying to. We have already noted that the requirements of medical school admissions are academic ability, motivation for medicine, and personal attributes such as teamwork and communication skills.

Personal attributes vs academic ability

However, at the moment in medicine there is a spectrum of opinion on what makes a good potential medical student. The two ends of the spectrum seem to be personal attributes and academic ability. At one end is the belief that what fundamentally makes a good doctor are good communication skills, empathy and teamwork, and that the science and knowledge element can be taught at medical school and further in postgraduate training. Those most firmly at the end of this spectrum are the more PBL-based medical schools. The other school of thought maintains that academic ability is the most important requisite of a doctor, and people's natural communication skills and empathy can be refined and taught at medical school. The furthest along this end of the spectrum are the traditional courses at Oxbridge, followed at a distance by some of the integrated schools in London such as UCL.

Of course, all parties are in agreement that both skills are eventually needed, and also that all students will possess some of both characteristics to a certain degree. In practice this means that no personal statement should focus on one side to the exclusion of the other. However, altering the balance and the focus to suit the particular type of medical school you are applying for will allow you to make the most of the section and catch the eye of interviewers. It also means that the 'one size fits all' advice you might have read elsewhere is not as useful as it might seem, as personal statements can and should be intelligently tailored to suit your audience.

This leaves the question of whether you should apply for the various different types of medical school in one UCAS application. The honest answer is that it would be difficult to construct a personal statement that suits them both. I would urge you to carefully consider which type of medical school you are suited to, and apply to the types that are appropriate for you. It is reasonable to mix PBL with integrated, or traditional with integrated, but joining the ends of the spectrum together may well play against your chances and is therefore not recommended.

'The kind of student I would love is the kind who bought his first chemistry set at the age of 10, and was hooked ever since.'

Oxbridge admissions tutor

'We want people who can speak to patients like a real human being, and not a robot or a preacher.'

PBL school admissions tutor

Along with these two ends of the spectrum, the other attributes that are generally sought by admissions tutors are teamwork, leadership, commitment, communication skills, empathy and motivation for medicine. One problem that recurs year on year is that there are common misconceptions of what each attribute actually entails. A rich understanding of what each of these attributes means is the best basis to write a personal statement that showcases these qualities in yourself. A detailed explanation of each attribute can be found below.

The personal attributes

Communication skills

THE 'ALL ABOUT' SYNDROME

When asked what communication skills are, many students respond in the following fashion: 'It's all about using your voice, how you talk to the patient, as well as things like body language and tone.'

Communication is a two-way street, with both an input and an output of data. Therefore a good communicator needs to develop all aspects of this attribute. A skilful command of language will be helpful both in interpreting what is being communicated and in phrasing a suitable reply. Organization skills are important in arranging information into an order that facilitates understanding in the recipient. Knowledge of popular culture, literature and current affairs facilitates the use and understanding of analogies. The bottom line is that body language, tone and speech are important, but communication is 'all about' dealing with information, and all elements – input, processing and output – should be considered.

How then can we demonstrate our understanding of this to the admissions tutors via our personal statement? The best approach is to show some of the skills we have discussed above. One of the steps of communication is input, which is to say under-standing what they want from you. By understanding the different focuses of types of medical school, you can customize your personal statement to suit what the reader is looking for from a candidate, demonstrating that you understand the 'question' of the personal statement. To demonstrate your output skills, your written English should be immaculate, and a moderate rhetorical flourish can be employed to underline your prowess in this regard.

Written structure

A well-organized personal statement will demonstrate that you are able to present information in a systematic fashion that makes it easier to follow. Students who can demonstrate originality in their structure may come across particularly well, as long as the structure has some reasoning behind it and is explained. You could, for example, arrange your personal statement into sections by personal attribute, demonstrating each in turn (see later in this chapter). Other inventive approaches include one student who chose to use Darwin's survival model to show how he was the 'fittest' for medical school.

Activities

In terms of content, activities such as acting, singing or public speaking can be an example of practising and developing communication skills, particularly in the output department. However, writing a speech may also show organizational skills, and participating in debate puts heavy demands on the input, processing and output skills of a student. Activities that involve person-to-person contact, particularly with age groups other than your own, will also help to develop communication skills. Such activities help a person understand the range of language and knowledge needed to be an effective communicator. This is also true of activities such as dancing, in which you have to communicate in a non-verbal manner. It is a misconception that admissions tutors frown upon non-mainstream activities, and although they may not enjoy watching a breakdancing show, they do appreciate that art and com-munication take many forms. Interviewers have stated that they will tend to ask students if they list nonconformist pastimes partly to see if they can discuss the benefits of the activity intelligently, and partly because they find such candidates genuinely interesting.

How to

'As a member of the school model UN debating team, I have had the chance to practise my communication skills as well as learn by observing others. I had to collate the relevant information, organize our arguments and express them expediently and accurately, which are skills I imagine will be useful in communicating with patients in my future career.'

Teamwork

'ALL ABOUT HELPING EACH OTHER OUT'

The next most frequent misconception held by students is what they understand by the term 'teamwork'. In mock and real interviews, as well as in descriptions on personal statements, many applicants talk about teamwork in the following manner or similar: 'Teamwork is all about helping each other out. Communication skills are the key to good teamwork. I've played in the school netball team, and also worked in a team of six girls on the school newsletter, and by working together on problems we can solve them more quickly.'

As with communication skills, students typically describe only some of the aspects of teamwork. While there is a degree of communication skill needed for good teamwork, knowledge and understanding of your role within the team, and execution of that role with diligence and skill, are the mainstay of good teamwork. If we take the example of basketball, if people are too keen to help a teammate who is defending a player, you will end up 'double teaming' one player, leaving another one open to score. The ideal situation is that each player will stick to their own role of marking one player, and do a good job of it. However, there are circumstances where double teaming can be helpful – for example, if an opposing player is particularly skilled, it might be necessary to help out your teammate, but this is the exception rather than the rule.

Therefore the important parts of teamwork are understanding your role, executing it with skill and diligence, and helping others appropriately when the situation requires. It also involves recognizing your own limitations and asking for help under the correct circumstances – it stands to reason that in a team, in order for someone to give help, someone must require it, and it is important to recognize that you may be the giver or receiver, and both are important. If you consider a kind-hearted doctor on the wards, he might help out a nurse who is escorting a patient to the bathroom, and pick up the phone for a busy ward clerk or bring some blood results down to the lab when no one is available to take them. However, if he does too many of these things he may be neglecting his own role of undertaking clinical history and examination, making diagnoses and initiating treatment. This would be detrimental to the healthcare team as a whole if it went on continuously.

How can we demonstrate this understanding of teamwork, and that we have this attribute? The best way to show the admissions tutors your understanding and possession of teamwork is to discuss the activities that involve groups such as sports teams, orchestras, Young Enterprise, Duke of Edinburgh's Award scheme, organizing school clubs, etc. You can then relate your experience to the elements of teamwork discussed above, ensuring that you cover the dimensions of teamwork discussed.

How to

'For my Duke of Edinburgh's gold award, I participated as both a team member, route planning for the group, and also as leader for a day, which involved navigating the team to the proposed destination. Playing violin as a member of the school orchestra and choir has given me an insight into the importance of commitment and teamwork in a musical context.'

Detail your contribution to each part of the activity. It is helpful to demonstrate your participation in teamwork in a variety of settings that give you greater experience in working with different groups of people and dynamics.

Leadership

There is an even greater burden of knowledge when it comes to leadership. Leadership involves communication skills, expert knowledge in the activity you are leading, the ability to delegate appropriately, conflict resolution skills and morale building. It is also important to be humble in your claims about leadership, as you will still be a young student.

How not to

'As a competent leader, I captain the archery team in school.'

You are declaring yourself to be a competent leader based on this one fact. I am not sure that admissions tutors would consider this as materially evident to the degree that you have stated it.

How to

'I have begun to learn about leadership by captaining the archery team.'

This not only demonstrates your achievement but also gives the impression that you understand the scale of your achievement in the context of the application, and life, and that you are modest and keen to learn more.

Commitment

Commitment is best demonstrated by long or difficult pursuit of a goal, and usually this manifests itself as an extra-curricular goal. It can be helpful to cite examples of high achievement that by definition would require effort and ability beyond that of an ordinary individual. However, commitment can be to a cause, philosophy or group of people, and long-standing voluntary work undertakings, organizing charitable events or supporting a cause, such as by letter-writing for Amnesty International, are all useful ways to show your commitment.

How to

'One of my greatest learning experiences is my career in competitive basketball. I played for my school and the Combined School team, winning several national championships and awards. But to me, basketball was more than just the medals. I distinctly recall the quarter-final match when our star player tore her anterior cruciate ligament. We struggled through the final matches to clinch the gold, but it was my teammate's pain that struck a chord in my heart – even more excruciating to her than her injured knee was the agony of helplessly watching us fight through sweat and tears.'

Empathy and sympathy

Empathy is an important attribute for a doctor, and is often the motivation for undertaking the arduous training and work. Empathy may be defined as 'trying to understand the feelings of others'.

Sympathy suggests caring for another's situation. Both are important for a doctor whose job is to care for others (sympathy), which is often best achieved by understanding patients (empathy).

Activities demonstrating empathy include voluntary work and work experience where you have a connection with others and try to effect a small change for the better in their lives.

How to

'I visit a lady who is partially blind on a weekly basis, as part of the 60-plus volunteering programme. In these sessions I help her with reading and other tasks that she would otherwise find difficult. Through this experience I have learned about communicating with adults and to forge links with the local community. I feel I have a greater understanding of the frustrations that the elderly can sometimes experience when they can no longer perform tasks with the same ease as before.'

Reflective learning: 'I feel I have a greater understanding' is an example of reflection, and is more humble and academically cautious than 'I have a greater understanding'. This student has not only reported her activity, but also identified how this experience affected her. By raising the point about the 'frustrations that the elderly can sometimes experience', she is demonstrating discovering something that can only really be gained from participation in the activity. This adds value to her personal statement and showcases her written communication skills.

Motivation for medicine

Admissions tutors are mostly united in agreeing that motivation for medicine is one of the important criteria in the admissions process. They also note that it is best assessed as part of the interview. This is due to the fact that it is the most difficult criterion to gauge accurately. Therefore it is almost impossible to launch a convincing argument for or against a candidate based on their UCAS personal statement alone. The idea of a seamless application arises from this point, in that the personal statement can be used to set up your interview, by giving strong topics for the panel to question you about – such as your work experience and research interests. However, sounding genuinely motivated is vital in achieving the call to interview.

First, an understanding of what is involved in the study of medicine, followed by the practice, is critical to maintaining a true interest; it is more difficult to convince someone that you are very enthusiastic about an activity you know little about. The aim of your 'motivation for medicine' section of the personal statement is to be genuine and interesting enough to merit a call for interview, where this interest will be further explored.

How to

'However, I think what makes me really different is my enthusiasm. I actually care about science. When my contemporaries were doing musical or sporting activities, I chose to be a research assistant because I was interested in the work. I undertook a laboratory research project on cancer cell signalling with the MRC outside school primarily for intellectual curiosity. I believe that people excel in their interests and my passion makes me a good candidate for you.'

This is an excellent example of expressed motivation, focused on a traditional school application. It demonstrates a journey of active choices to pursue a chosen interest with vigour. The concluding sentence ties it all together and puts forward a case for calling the applicant to interview to further discuss their interest.

Putting it all together: how to construct your personal statement

'Classic' structure: integrated

- Introduction: interest in medicine.

- Academics: discussion of biology and chemistry.

- Work experience and voluntary work.

- Extra-curricular activities.

- Conclusion about motivation for medicine.

This is the most common format for personal statements and most of the personal statements I review each year have this as the backbone of their structure. The advantages are that admissions tutors will be familiar with it, and they will know what to expect in each section. If you particularly excel in certain areas, then these will be highlighted relative to other students' applications, as your achievements will stand out in direct comparison to what else tutors are seeing.

- This format allows you to use your extra-curricular activities to illustrate some of the personal attributes sought by admissions tutors.

- The format can be adapted to lean more towards either a traditional or PBL style, by adjusting the amounts of scientific or personal-attribute material included.

- This format is best suited for an integrated medical school application as it is the most balanced of the three common formats.

Integrated course-orientated personal statement

I have always been fascinated by many branches of science. I especially enjoy the relationship between biology and chemistry, and how biochemical reactions underpin activities of the human body. What drew me to medicine in particular was the combination of the scientific appeal and, more important, the application of this method in a humanitarian manner. My ambition is to earn the opportunity to be responsible for the health of many people and be trusted by them every day.

To explore more about the medical profession, I have been working as a volunteer in the orthopaedic ward of my local hospital every week for two years now. I have enjoyed this opportunity very much and my most lasting memory is a conversation with an ex-footballer who has sadly become a double amputee. Simply engaging him in conversation and allowing him to talk lifted his spirits, which gave me a taste of the empathy on which the medical profession is founded. I also had a placement in the hospital, which enabled me to observe doctors from different departments, including A&E, CT scanning, MRI unit, endoscopy and the main theatres. This opportunity helped me to gain an insight into the various aspects of a career in medicine and begin to appreciate the contrasts between specialties.

I decided to take a gap year to pursue a dream of travelling the world while gaining practical medical experience. So far I have undertaken some placements, in particular at a nursing home and a residential home, in order to become familiar with the similarities as well as the differences between such environments. I am beginning to understand that the patient journey through the hospital both begins and ends in the community. I intend to take advantage of my travels to explore the healthcare systems of other countries, by undertaking work placements in hospitals abroad, starting with the respiratory medicine department in a Romanian hospital, and also in Iran where I will spend time in a GP clinic to widen my perspective on medicine as a whole. I will also be continuing my scientific education by assisting with research at the MRC, and working as an assistant in various laboratories within a hospital, which will give me an insight into integrating science with interpersonal interaction. I am greatly looking forward to immersing myself in other foreign environments in the USA, Sweden and Turkey.

I served as the head of the school council for three years, and by representing the student body at meetings with the headmaster and school governors, I experienced the roles of both leader and team player in a challenging environment.

During my A levels, I participated as a teaching assistant in mathematics classes aimed at pupils in the lower years of my school, which encouraged my own patience and ability to explain concepts clearly and concisely. I now tutor schoolchildren after school and I feel this is continuing to further develop these attributes.

Outside my studies, I am interested in politics and philosophy, and follow closely the Middle Eastern and especially the Iranian political scene. I am also a keen sportsman, with a particular passion for football, in which I represent a local and community team, and which is a discipline I hope to continue at university level.

I have enjoyed taking part in many academic competitions. I passed the first round of the Physics Olympiad in both the UK and in Iran. I achieved two gold certificates in the senior mathematics challenge as well as a distinction in the Olympiad. In chemistry, I represented the school in practical-orientated RSC competition, in addition to earning a silver certificate in the Olympiad.

Alternative A: academic style

- Interest in science and academia.

- Interest in biological science.

- Interest in medicine.

- Extra-curricular activities.

- Conclusion.

    - This is best suited for traditional medical school application.

    - It gives ample room for you to discuss how your scientific interests developed over time. It then allows you to focus more on the medical perspective and why medicine appeals to you.

Traditional course-orientated personal statement

Drawn by its intriguing title, I read a book called The Man Who Mistook His Wife for a Hat *by Oliver Sacks. I not only enjoyed looking into the range of unusual neurological disorders but also into how the patients coped and gained skills from their disabilities – as, for example, in the story called 'Witty Ticcy Ray', about a man suffering from severe Tourette's syndrome, who had bursts of wild musical creativity from his tics and went on to become a successful jazz drummer. I found this book very interesting because Dr Sacks presents the patients rather than just the disorders, and shows the aspects of the illnesses that are not usually taught academically.*

It is not only the complexity of the mind that intrigues me, but also the complexity of the human body. I am fascinated by the way each cell has a specific role and how they are constantly working together to allow the body to function as a whole organism. There are always new things to discover about the human body, and I look forward to studying medicine in order to increase my understanding of it. While studying the AS biology course, the topic that I found the most stimulating was the study of the heart. I read an excerpt of Guyton and Hall's Medical Physiology *and I realized that while we were only taught that the coordination of contraction is regulated by the sinoatrial node, heart muscle actually has its own intrinsic contractility at a lower rate.*

This introduction to the personal statement is eye-catching and unusual. It is well designed to highlight first and foremost the attributes sought by traditional schools, which are scientific interest and ability. It is substantive and discusses specific examples to help convince the reader of a deep-seated and genuine interest. It gives the impression of a student who not only enjoys the science that they are taught but seeks out more. This *unsatisfied* intellectual curiosity is an important quality to demonstrate to selectors. It indicates that the candidate has not yet reached their full potential and is eager to learn.

Alternative B: personal attribute style

- Interest in medicine: including discussion of personal attributes required of medicine.

- Motivation for medicine: work experience or voluntary work.

- Commitment.

- Teamwork.

- Communication skills.

- Leadership.

- Empathy.

- Conclusion.

  - This structure leans more towards PBL-based medical schools.

  - It gives a stronger focus on the personal attributes, and will clearly cover each one with a illustrative example.

  - It is less focused on academic interest, although this may be covered more briefly in the introduction.

PBL medical school-orientated personal statement

Once all this is done, it is time to write about this very process, which is how you came to discover that you have this motivation. Other attributes that you will also wish to demonstrate are teamwork, leadership and communication skills. If you are applying for medicine, you will be expecting to obtain a minimum of ABB at A level, which already puts you in a self-selected group that has a good baseline in science. The important thing to remember is that admissions tutors for PBL schools consider most of the academic information to be obtained from GCSE, AS-level and medical school examination marks. This leaves your personal statement and interview to reveal the other attributes as discussed above. Interest in science is different from academic ability, and it is worth touching on, although it should not be the main focus of your personal statement.

> *My interest in medicine stems from a wish to be involved in a practical application of science and a desire to help people in a direct, hands-on and skilled fashion. In order to clarify my view of the medical profession, I have undertaken work experiences in the UK, Europe and Far East, and attended the Medlink conference in Nottingham, and I feel that this has given me a realistic yet optimistic perspective on life as a doctor. In my opinion there is no other occupation in which I could help people more, or take more personal pride in.*
>
> *I see the personal requisites of the medical profession as fivefold; empathy, communication, leadership, teamwork and dedication. Volunteering at the Lady Skinner Ward in Charing Cross Hospital and helping the elderly during their rehabilitation helped to develop compassion and a sense of duty to society in me, both facets of a caring nature.*
>
> *I discovered that communication skills were vital as a senior prefect at my school, which required the organization of 130 other prefects in their duties. I developed my language skills as the producer of the sixth-form newsletter, What's Going On?, both in terms of writing articles and in managing the team of writers and editor. As the marketing director of the Young Enterprise company, Get IT, I liaised, delegated and collaborated with my team over the promotion of the product, an academic revision guide written by and for students.*

I feel that my leadership skills have developed most in challenging environments, which I encountered teaching English at an orphanage in Malaysia. The children had difficulty in comprehending the value of their studies, and it was only by leading the group, planning a timetable with them and talking about my own experiences in studies that I could break through and motivate the children to success.

In my involvement in the Duke of Edinburgh's Award scheme expeditions, I found that teamwork involved executing my own duties, such as navigation, to the best of my ability, as well as assisting the team by offering to share the tent loads when people were quietly struggling.

I have represented the school team and received school colours for rowing, and I hope that the mental strength and stamina that I have been developing will be useful in my medical studies. I achieved a black belt in Shotokan karate at the age of 15, trained in the Wong Fei Hong martial arts academy in China and performed on Chinese television, and throughout my time spent in martial arts the underlying message is of self-improvement through dedication.

My interests include studying Chinese and classical philosophy, for which I attend Ealing Chinese School and the Classics Society at school. I am interested in Manga and Japanese animation and enjoy reading the background of its development and cultural influences. I also enjoy badminton, in which I am the school captain and represent the borough of Hammersmith and Fulham.

School reference

The school reference is an important piece of subjective evidence for admissions tutors to use to assess personal attributes that are more difficult to judge from the personal statement. In particular, dedication and motivation for medicine may be demonstrated, as well as professional behaviours such as punctuality and conduct. A good reference is another foundation building block of a solid application; more importantly, a negative reference can be disastrous for your chances of success. As with all the steps, there is no easy solution, and you will have to earn it over a period of time. However, support from your teachers cannot be earned overnight. A chronically poor student with a bad attitude will find it difficult to change this impression simply by 'sucking up' to the relevant teacher for the duration of the application process. However, a genuine endeavour to turn over a new leaf and start with a clean, attentive, punctual attitude will be appreciated and may convince your teacher that you have the right qualities to study medicine.

Things to consider

Read through your school reports to identify any problems that your teachers have picked up on. In particular, look out for any subtle references that you are, or come across as, arrogant, and if there are any, think about ways you could reduce this impression.

Schoolteachers who have helped other students through their process of application will also be a helpful port of call, and once you have decided on making your decision to apply for medicine it may be helpful to register this interest with your form tutor or appropriate subject teacher, such as your biology or chemistry teacher. This will be useful for whoever is writing your reference, as they can genuinely refer to your long-standing interest in medicine. Judiciously keeping them updated with your achievements will help to keep them 'in the loop' and form a partnership in your application.

Things to avoid

Simple things like handing in coursework, homework or even administrative paperwork late will reflect badly on you and your organizational ability. Avoiding any disciplinary issues with school goes without saying. All these activities are not simply to make a good impression; as we have discussed all along, the paper tiger is not what we are crafting here – a good doctor will genuinely be prompt.

Other qualities you might expect from your doctor would include cleanliness, diligence and excellent time management. Do not underestimate the impact of bad handwriting on your career; medical notes that are poorly written are both a nightmare for colleagues and a genuine hazard for patient care. Similarly, essays and homework written in scrawl are unlikely to win the approval of the teacher who writes your reference, so if this is a problem for you it is worth working on now. Lateness or absences will also reflect badly, and if these are problems for you, it may be prudent to consider how to change these practices. Lateness to the job as a doctor might mean a whole clinic list of patients being delayed an hour each, and yourself and the nursing staff working over lunchtime, or it might mean that you are not present for a cardiac arrest on the ward at five minutes past 9 am, with serious consequences.

Discuss with the teacher who will write your reference what general areas they will be covering, so that you can coordinate and not duplicate the achievements listed. Several teachers I have spoken to have said that they would prefer the student to have a straightforward approach in discussing the reference, rather than trying to influence the teacher in a roundabout manner. Be upfront, polite and humble, and the teachers will do their best to support your application.

In summary, therefore, things to consider here are:

- Register your interest with the teacher writing your reference as early as possible.

- Ask for their advice and guidance.

- Update them on any significant achievements.

- Perform well in class as well as in exams and tests.

Things to avoid here are:

- Disciplinary issues.

- Poor handwriting.

- Lateness.

- Unkempt/untidy appearance.

- Faked or excessive enthusiasm about your application.

- Arrogant behaviour.

Oxbridge applications

With regard to Oxbridge applications, many schools have specific policies on these. Oxford and Cambridge colleges will not usually accept two students from the same school for the same subject in the same year, so applicants for medicine are commonly asked to select their college of preference early on. It is therefore important to research on the colleges and register this interest with the school so that you will not be clashing with other students.

Teachers may not recommend everyone to apply for Oxbridge so that they can fully support those whom they are recommending. Applying against the recommendation of the school is certainly possible but it is important to take on board the advice that they offer, considering that it is founded on years of experience.

Summary

- Medical schools lie along a bipolar spectrum in terms of what they are looking for from candidates.

- Use this information to your advantage to tailor your application towards the type of school you are aiming for.

- For traditional schools, focus on an interest in science and intellectual curiosity.

- For PBL schools, focus on personal attributes and motivation for medicine.

- For all statements, make sure you cover all other areas which are not the main focus.

- Use specific examples of events, reflections or short anecdotes to substantiate your extra-curricular activities.

- Creativity can be demonstrated in organization and structure, so long as it follows an obvious or explained pattern.

- A good school reference must be earned, which is a long-term goal.

- Discuss your interest in medicine, activities and application with your referring teacher as soon as possible.

CHAPTER 6

Medical school examinations: UKCAT and BMAT

How this chapter will help you get into medical school

As we have seen in Chapter 3, academic ability is one of the key attributes sought in potential medical students. A specific medical admissions examination has been desired by some medical schools which felt that A levels were not an effective discriminator for top students, as there were increasing numbers of students achieving top grades.

This chapter will give you examples of what you will be facing in the examinations. It provides tips for preparation and guidance to further resources to use to maximize your mark and thereby your chances for admission.

UKCAT

UKCAT (UK Clinical Aptitude Test) is used by many universities as one of the indicators of suitability for entry to medical school. As requirements change each year, it is important to check if your university requires it, but the list is far longer than that for BMAT (just four). The examination takes place in July, typically after AS levels for most applicants.

UKCAT consists of five sections:

- Verbal reasoning.

- Decision analysis.

- Quantitative reasoning.

- Abstract reasoning.

- Non-cognitive analysis.

There is an element of performance pressure in the UKCAT, which consists of 175 questions to answer in two hours, so in the acute setting, being fresh and ready for the questions is vital to performance. Some example questions for each section are included below; these are taken from *How to Master the UKCAT* by Mike Bryon and Jim Clayden, published by Kogan Page (2010).

Verbal reasoning

The verbal reasoning sub-test comprises a series of passages followed by questions. Each question is a statement and your task is to decide whether, according to the passage, the statement is true or false or if you cannot tell if it is true or false. Typically these questions require you to comprehend meaning and significance, assess logical strength, identify valid inference, distinguish between a main idea and a subordinate one, recognize the writer's intention and identify a valid summary, interpretation or conclusion. Some examples of typical questions are below.

Passage 1

Towns that have become commuter and second-home hotspots are valued for their housing stock, schools and unspoilt civic centres. It is now possible for working families to relocate away from cities without affecting their earning power. Commuting three days a week and working from home the rest has meant that many more people are willing to give up the city life and move to more rural areas to fulfil their dream of homes with gardens and cricket on the green. So many metropolitan dwellers have made the move that property prices in the more popular locations have become amongst the most expensive in the country.

1   New technology is the reason why it is possible for working families to relocate without affecting their earning power.

   True   False   Cannot tell

                                           Answer [   ]

2   The only reason for these locations becoming so popular is only due to commuting even if for just part of the week.

True   False   Cannot tell

Answer _____

3   An idea of an unspoilt civic centre could include, along with cricket on the green, a traditional high street with local shops.

True   False   Cannot tell

Answer _____

Passage 2

Asparagus is a perennial and wild asparagus is found growing in light, well-drained soil across Europe, northern Africa and central Asia. People from all over the world enjoy eating it. The most sought-after domesticated varieties are from Canada and they prefer a soil with a pH of around 6.5. The domesticated varieties grow best in a humus-rich medium and will then each produce around half a kilo of crop. In the spring the plant sends up the spears that if left will open to form new foliage, but for the first six weeks of each season these are cut when they are around 10 centimetres tall. After the cutting season the spears are allowed to mature so that the plants can re-establish themselves. The spears of the cultivated varieties are far thicker than those that grow in the wild and the crown (the shallow root ball) much larger, but the flavour of wild asparagus is superior. In the autumn the female plants fruit to produce small inedible berries.

4   All asparagus plants like a soil with a pH of 6.5.

True   False   Cannot tell

Answer _____

5   It can be inferred from the passage that when the author describes the fruit as inedible he means that humans can't eat it.

True   False   Cannot tell

Answer _____

6   Asparagus only grows in Europe, northern Africa and central Asia.

True   False   Cannot tell

Answer _____

Answers

1   *Answer:* Cannot tell

    Explanation: The passage states that it is now possible to relocate without affecting earning power but the reason for this new development is not given in the passage. It might be because of new technology but we cannot rule out the possibility that there are other causes; for example, the reason might be that it is the introduction of new legislation that allows workers a better work–life balance. Because we cannot establish new technology as the reason we must conclude that we cannot tell if the statement is true or false.

2   *Answer:* False

    Explanation: Two reasons for the increase in popularity are mentioned in the passage, and although the passage dwells mainly on one of them, commuter towns, the issue of second-home hotspots is also raised as a reason for the increase in popularity.

3   *Answer:* True

    Explanation: This is a tough question, so don't be too hard on yourself if you got it wrong. Although the passage does not mention a traditional high street with local shops, it is reasonable to conclude that this concept might form part of 'an idea of an unspoilt civic centre'. The statement starts with 'an idea' not 'the idea' and states it 'could include' not 'does or should include'. These are weak assertions and allow for many possibilities and for this reason the correct answer is true.

4   *Answer:* Cannot tell

    Explanation: The passage states that the most sought-after domesticated varieties prefer a pH of 6.5, but we cannot tell or infer from the information given if other varieties of wild asparagus also share this characteristic.

5   *Answer:* True

    Explanation: Inedible means indigestible, unpalatable or poisonous. It is not expressly stated in the passage that the berries are indigestible, unpalatable or poisonous for humans but if we look to the context of the passage then it is clear that we can infer this information. The passage is about asparagus and its edible spears and it is stated that people all over the world enjoy eating them. The context of the passage therefore is asparagus and people growing it or picking it to eat. Given this context we can infer that the berries are inedible for humans. It might be that the berries are inedible for other species too but we cannot infer this from the passage.

6   *Answer:* False

    Explanation: The passage states that wild asparagus grows in Europe, northern Africa and central Asia but it also states that cultivated asparagus grows in Canada, so we can infer that the statement is false.

Decision analysis

These tests are about making good judgements in less than ideal circumstances – as is often the case in real life. The information provided is deliberately incomplete and the rules being followed are deliberately ambiguous. It is your task to decipher the code and then decide which of the suggested answers are best. You have to do this within a tight time frame.

Questions

Codes

Modifiers

321. Parallel	324. Lessen
322. Append	325. Akin
323. Reverse	

Features and instructions

601. Elevated	606. Add
602. Temperate	607. Delete
603. Tiny	608. Inflation
604. Popular	609. Deflation
605. Unfashionable	

Lexis

930. Service	937. Pasta
931. Commodity	938. Mobile phone contract
932. Wide-screen TV	939. Refrigerator
933. Milk	940. Wooden flooring
934. Cigarettes	941. Gasoline
935. Banking	942. Soft furnishings
936. Landscape gardening	943. The basket of goods and services

1 606 937, 934 321 607

    A Delete cigarettes and add pasta.

    B Add cigarettes and delete pasta.

    C Add pasta and delete cigarettes.

    D Remove cigarettes and add pasta.

Answer [   ]

2   942, 324 607, 604, 321 601, 608

   A Soft furnishings are popular but they experience high inflation.

   B Soft furnishings are very popular but consider deleting them as they suffer very high inflation.

   C Think about deleting soft furnishings; while popular, they have high inflation.

   D Don't delete soft furnishings; though they experience inflation they remain very popular.

Answer [＿＿＿＿＿＿]

Answers

1   *Answer:* D

   Explanation: The code reads add pasta, cigarettes parallel delete. A and C could be right but for the modifier 32, which means parallel. A parallel is a sort of synonym, and only answer D offers a parallel to delete = remove.

2   *Answer:* C

   Explanation: The code reads soft furnishings, lessen delete, popular, parallel elevated, inflation. Lessen delete can be to 'think about or consider deleting' (but it can't be 'don't delete'). Parallel elevated can be high or very high. The code for popular is unmodified, so very popular is not the best suggestion. This leaves only suggested answer C as correct and including all the codes.

Quantitative reasoning

The test consists of 40 multiple-choice questions divided up into 10 blocks of 4 questions for which you will have 22 minutes, ie approximately 2 minutes per block, or 30 seconds per question. As there are no penalties for incorrect answers, you have nothing to lose by guessing answers if you are short of time towards the end.

Questions

Questions 1 to 4 concern the population of a certain town which can be divided into the following age groups:

Age group	Population
0–4	6,450
5–9	7,600
10–14	8,450
15–19	7,400
20–24	5,550
25–29	6,150
30–34	8,100
35–39	8,750
40–44	8,450
45–49	8,400
50–54	10,150
55–59	9,600
60–64	7,950
65–69	7,450
70–74	7,100
75–79	6,450
80–84	4,500
85–89	2,750

1 How many people are younger than 20?

A 5,550

B 7,400

C 29,000

D 29,900

E 30,000

Answer

2 If the total population is 131,250, approximately what percentage are under 25?

A 10%

B 15%

C 20%

D 25%

E 30%

Answer

3   If everyone retires at 65, what fraction of the population is within 10 years of retirement?

   A 1/4

   B 1/5

   C 1/7

   D 1/10

   E 1/20

   Answer [   ]

4   What is the ratio of schoolchildren (5–19) to retired people (65+)?

   A 4 : 5

   B 4 : 3

   C 1 : 1

   D 2 : 1

   E 1 : 2

   Answer [   ]

Questions 5 to 8 concern the television viewing of children in a town in the east of the country and a town in the west:

East		West	
Child	**Minutes**	**Child**	**Minutes**
A	95	K	145
B	78	L	70
C	91	M	102
D	87	N	121
E	65	O	109
F	71	P	89
G	92	Q	96
H	69	R	113
I	82	S	121
J	80	T	98

5   What is the average viewing time for a child in the east?

   A 82.3

   B 91.0

   C 79.9

D 81.5

E 81.0

Answer [ ]

6   What is the median viewing time for a child in the east?

A 80

B 81

C 82

D 80.4

E 81.7

Answer [ ]

7   How does the range of the viewing times for the west compare with the east?

A The mode is greater.

B The median is greater.

C It is smaller.

D It is twice as big.

E It is two-and-a-half times greater.

Answer [ ]

8   What is the mode of the viewing times in the west?

A 75

B 106.4

C 121

D 105.5

E 145

Answer [ ]

Answers

1   *Answer:* D. 29,900. Skill set: Table reading, addition
     6,450 + 7,600 + 8,450 + 7,400 = 29,900.

2   *Answer:* D. 25%. Skill set: Table reading, addition, percentages
     6,450 + 7,600 + 8,450 + 7,400 + 5,550 = 35,450, (35,450/131,250) = 0.270,
     therefore approximately 25%.

3   *Answer:* C. 1/7. Skill set: Table reading, fractions
     9,600 + 7,950 = 17,550, (17,550/131,250) = 0.134, approximately 1/7.

4 *Answer:* A. 4 : 5. Skill set: Table reading, addition, ratios
Schoolchildren: 7,600 + 8,450 + 7,400 = 23,450; retired: 7,450 + 7,100 + 6,450 + 4,500 + 2,750 = 28,250. The ratio 23,450 : 28,250 is about 4 : 5.

5 *Answer:* E. 81.0. Skill set: Table reading, mean
Add up all the times = 810; then divide by the number of children, 10. 810/10 = 81.0.

6 *Answer:* B. 81. Skill set: Table reading, median
Put the numbers in numerical order; then take the number in the middle. As there is an even number, split the difference between the two central numbers, 80 and 82, giving 81.

7 *Answer:* E. Two-and-a-half times greater. Skill set: Table reading, range
Range in east = 95 − 65 = 30, range in west 145 − 70 = 75. 75/30 = 2.5.

8 *Answer:* C. 121. Skill set: Table reading, mode
Mode is the most frequent. There are two occurrences of 121.

Abstract reasoning

The abstract reasoning sub-test is intended to assess ability to identify patterns among abstract shapes. It does this is by asking the candidate to identify to which group a particular shape or set of shapes belongs.

For each set A and set B there will be five items, and you have to click on one of the buttons, A, B or C, to indicate whether you think the test shape belong to set A, set B, or neither.

Questions

1

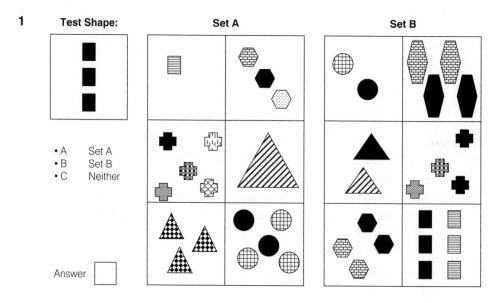

Test Shape:

- A   Set A
- B   Set B
- C   Neither

Answer

Set A

Set B

2   **Test Shape:**   **Set A**   **Set B**

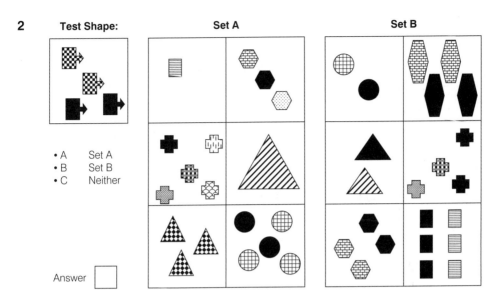

- A   Set A
- B   Set B
- C   Neither

Answer ☐

Answers

Set A has an odd number of shapes and fewer black ones than shaded.
Set B has an even number of shapes and the same number of black as shaded.

1 C

2 B

Non-cognitive analysis

The fifth sub-test that makes up the UKCAT is very different in nature from the other four. In fact, it is not a test in the usual sense but more a questionnaire, and it is scored very differently from the other sub-tests. Its stated aim is to expand the range of information available on candidates by providing a report on attributes and characteristics regarding the candidate's personal style. Take this to mean that the assessors will use your responses to build a psychometric profile of your attitude and personality. You have 30 minutes in which to complete this section of the UKCAT and you are required to consider a list of statements and indicate your personal response to each of them.

Questions

1   Given the fact that healthcare must be rationed I reluctantly conclude that someone who engages in high-risk activities can't expect the same level of medical care as someone who lives life more moderately.

A   I agree with this conclusion.

B   Generally I agree with this conclusion.

C   Generally I would not agree with this conclusion.

D   I particularly agree with this conclusion.

E   I do not particularly agree with this conclusion.

Answer _____

2   I struggle to pay attention to small detail.

A   I totally disagree with the statement.

B   I don't agree with the statement.

C   I partially agree with the statement.

D   I agree with the statement.

E   I totally agree with the statement.

Answer _____

Answers

1   *Explanation:* That healthcare might need to be rationed does not imply that it should be rationed according to people's lifestyle and certain lifestyles should be discriminated against in terms of the level of care they receive.

2   *Explanation:* Your work in the health service will require extensive detail and small differences will make a significant difference to the quality of care that you provide. For these reasons an admission that you struggle to pay attention to small detail is unlikely to support your application.

BMAT

The BMAT (BioMedical Admissions Test) is a three-part paper used by Oxford, Cambridge and UCL.

The importance of the BMAT

BMAT scoring is a relative. Furthermore, each cohort is specific for each university, such that your BMAT score for UCL might be better than that for Oxford, if the Oxford cohort was better on average.

There are books and courses that will help you prepare for this examination, and although these are not recommended by the official BMAT website, there are several advantages that can be gained through practice, not least of which is discovering the gaps in your knowledge and thereby directing your revision. Practice of BMAT questions also encourages a deductive approach to scientific problems, and encourages students to think creatively about science. The essays might encourage students to think outside the syllabus box, but the science section encourages you to search the knowledge that you have and apply it in different ways. BMAT preparation will therefore not only help to improve your numerical score but will also develop approaches to scientific problem solving that will be useful in interview. However, there is no 'quick fix' or particular technique to scoring highly on the BMAT, and candidates looking for easy solutions by attending a weekend course without the requisite revision will not find their scores improving. Long-term preparation is the best solution.

Section 1

The first section is verbal reasoning. The best preparation is to get attuned to the particular nature of the test by practising questions. In addition to the sample questions available on the website (www.admissionstests.cambridgeassessment. org.uk/adt/bmat), try some of the practice questions below, taken from *How to Master the BMAT* by Chris John Tyreman, published by Kogan Page (2009).

Question

1   The nuclear industry claims that its power stations are safe and no threat to people. If this is true, then why do they locate their power plants away from population centres? By doing so they are admitting that nuclear power is potentially dangerous to local communities. Which one of the following, if true, would most seriously weaken the above argument?

A Reactors are located away from communities as part of a general risk management strategy.

B The potential for harm following any leak is significantly reduced.

C Cooling water for the reactors is not available in populated areas.

D Costs are lower and local communities are less likely to oppose planning applications.

Answer [   ]

Answer
1   C (C offers an alternative explanation to the (false) premise that nuclear reactors are sited away from population centres on safety grounds).

Section 2

The scientific questions only require GCSE-level knowledge, in order to put candidates on a level playing field by not disadvantaging students who do not take all science and maths AS or A levels. It is important to realize that your GCSE knowledge may have faded significantly without revision in the intervening year, so the first step is to go through it in fine detail. This particularly applies to any subjects that you may not be continuing to AS or A level, and for most students this is at least one discipline, commonly dropped because you may be less comfortable with it. It is also important to recap the GCSE content even in the subjects that you are currently studying, as AS/A2 material may not be relevant for the BMAT. For most students this will involve at least one subject.

The actual knowledge requirement is not great, but the idea of the BMAT is to test your application of this knowledge. Aside from helping you to become very familiar with the material, practice questions such as those below will help you hone your applied skills.

Questions

1   What is the power of an electric kettle if the heating element has a resistance of 23 ohm? Take mains voltage to be 230 volts.

A 2.2 kW

B 2.3 kW

C 2.5 kW

D 3 kW

E 1.5 kW

Answer

2   Silicon is found in group 14 of the periodic table.

$$^{28}_{14}\text{Si}$$

Silicon-30 is an isotope of silicon. Which of the following statements is true for silicon-30?

A 14 protons, 14 neutrons and 14 electrons.

B 14 protons, 16 neutrons and 14 electrons.

C 16 protons, 14 neutrons and 16 electrons.

D 30 neutrons plus protons and 16 electrons.

Answer

3   Most of the chemical digestion of carbohydrates, protein and fats takes place in which part of the gastro-intestinal tract catalysed by enzymes released by which gland(s)?

A Stomach and thyroid gland.

B Stomach and pancreas gland.

C Duodenum and adrenal glands.

D Small intestine and pancreas gland.

E Small intestine and pituitary gland.

Answer ⬚

4   Solve the inequality $x(2x + 6) \leq 8$.

A $x = 1; x = -4$

B $x \leq 1; x \leq -4$

C $4 \leq x \leq -1$

D $-4 \leq x \leq 1$

Answer ⬚

Answers

1   B (2.3 kW; $V = IR$, so $230 = I.23$ giving $I = 10$ ohm; power $= I.2R$).

2   B (atomic number $= 14$ protons $= 14$ electrons; atomic mass $=$ protons $+$ neutrons $= 30$; $30 - 14 = 16$ neutrons; only the number of neutrons changes in isotopes).

3   D (most nutrients are absorbed in the small intestine; the pancreas releases enzymes to speed up the breakdown of food and an alkaline fluid to neutralize stomach acid).

4   D ($-4 \leq x \leq 1$; $x(2x + 6) \leq 8$; i) $\cdot$ 2: gives $x(x + 3) \leq 4$; then ii) expand: $x2 + 3x \leq 4$; iii) re-arrange: $x2 + 3x - 4 \leq 0$; factorize: iv) $(x1)(x4)$, adding signs to give $(x - 1)(x + 4)$; finally sketch $y = x2 + 3x - 4$, using the roots from the factored expression, ie when $y = 0$, $x = +1$ or -4 and when $x = 0$, $y = -4$.

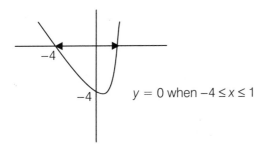

$y = 0$ when $-4 \leq x \leq 1$

Section 3

There is some controversy regarding Section 3, the essays. It was felt that it may favour public-school students who might have had greater exposure to unusual questions, and who, because of their greater experience, might therefore perform better, particularly with the structuring of the answers. Therefore in the current embodiment of the BMAT a suggested structure is included that usually follows the format of introduction and defining the problem, followed by advancing arguments for and against the statement, and concluding with a reasoned explanation of the candidate's own position.

The essay is most useful as a tool for eliminating candidates of poor ability rather than differentiating the top students from the rest of the pack. However, there is some variability of importance attached to the essay section from various universities, so bearing this in mind will allow you to focus your preparation for the BMAT appropriately.

Creativity is difficult to teach with examples in a formal way, as that would result in formulaic 'creative' answers, which would be somewhat of a paradox. I encourage an interest-driven approach to acquiring appropriate examples to discuss. Students can delve into learning resources from their regular curriculum, as well as additional reading they may have done around the subject. Reading scientific news and journals such as New Scientist and Student BMJ could be another source of interesting examples that could be used to fit their point.

Students often ask what to do when they run out of ideas, and rather than giving a source of answers I encourage them to use the following framework for synthesizing examples from the knowledge they already have. I refer to this as the creativity framework. Essentially, if you are lost for answers, think of possible exam questions by thinking through each of the science subjects in turn. Once you have exhausted these, think about the history of developments in, for example, biology or chemistry, and see if there are any useful examples there. After this, take your search further afield, to historical science figures, history, geography, politics and economics for ideas that will reinforce your essay. See the sample essay below for some excellent examples of 'out of the box' thinking.

The creativity framework is:

- biology;
- physics;
- chemistry;
- mathematics;
- the history of science or of scientific discovery;
- famous scientists;

- history;

- politics;

- economics;

- world events.

Cambridge considers the score of the essays less highly than Oxford and UCL, although there is some variability between colleges. This is because admissions tutors find that the essays have a prescribed structure that results in formulaic essays which are difficult to differentiate between. However, if you score poorly in the essays, it will count against you, and, as a rule of thumb, aiming for a minimum of 9.0 will give you the best chance of success. UCL in particular may discuss your BMAT essay and if it is one of your choices, it is critical to note down what you recall about your essay on the evening after the exam, so that you can reflect on your answer and speak intelligently about it at interview, which can be some months down the line.

HOW TO ANSWER ESSAY QUESTIONS

Below are an example BMAT essay question, an answer by a student in a mock exam, and an analysis of the essay.

EXAMPLE BMAT QUESTION

You have to know the past to understand the present.

Advance an argument in support of this statement. What arguments can you think of to refute this statement? Write a balanced conclusion.

STUDENT ANSWER

The author is saying that to know why the situation is how it is, we have to know the events that led up to it. Supporting this argument would be the imbalance of males and females in China. To understand why this is, you would have to know that in the past, the one-child policy was set up, and because of this, many parents killed their baby if one was a girl, so that they could have a boy. This was out of economic necessity as they could work in the field or earn money. Therefore to understand the gender imbalance in China, you would have to know the past. Another argument for this statement is that in Hiroshima and Nagasaki, people in the older generation who were survivors of the atomic bombs in the past may have a higher incidence of cancer. Thus, in order to understand the disease burden of the present, you have to understand the history of nuclear attacks in the past.

An argument against it would be the use of medicines, for example paracetamol. It is widely accepted and used even if most people do not know how it was found or made, or in this case they do not need to know the past to use it in the present. Also, another argument against this would be the use of Newton's laws of motion. Many people do not know their origins and discovery, but they still understand the concepts and make use of them, for example in friction when braking. In conclusion, although sometimes it is necessary to know the past of a situation to understand the present, in some circumstances the present can be accepted without knowing the past. Determining the course of our future, however, might be another story.

ANALYSIS

Introduction. Good interpretation of the quote. You are saying that 'past' means events leading up to the present, and you've not wasted any space or time on padding, which makes your introduction difficult to criticize.

First paragraph. Excellent first example. You are using a geography/history example, and it is well put such that it is watertight to criticism. Indeed, there are many reasons why one sex may be more numerous than another, but you must know about the one-child policy to see the main contributor. Furthermore, you go on to explain the significance and how this fact led to a decrease in females (don't forget the cultural significance of 'passing down the family name' too). I think this paragraph is tight, tidy and convincing. Very good.

The second example is the nuclear one (somehow nuclear technology or bombs are useful examples in several essays), but rather than a simple example, you have gone for a nice physics/biology example, where you explain about the effects of radiation (you could slip in the fact that ionizing radiation from the bombs causes direct damage to DNA, causing mutations, which may lead to cancer, in order to show off your scientific knowledge).

These are good examples, and you've covered a lot of bases in this time. The process of searching for examples from biology, chemistry, physics and history over time is often useful. I might have gone with 'The understanding of present scientific fact is often dependent on past discoveries, ie the knowledge of the atom and the electron led to the creation of the electron microscope, which later led to the discovery of cell organelles' (this uses history, chemistry, biology and physics, all in one!).

Second paragraph. Again you've done well with two quite different examples, the point of the first one being that you don't necessarily need to know the mechanism of a drug for it to be effective and for you to know that it is in fact effective (it may be preferable to know the mechanism of action, but there are some drugs where we simply don't, but trial data still show good effect).

Newton's laws of motion are another good one. With a poor sense of humour, I might have put 'people do not need to know that an apple fell on his head, to make use of his laws of motion in their everyday lives', but that's just me. I think your argument is well structured, and you have expressed the thought in a way that is academically cautious enough to withstand most criticism.

I might have mentioned the previous theory that the world was flat; we do not need to need to know that this was a prevailing theory to understand orbit calculations for our (very spherical) world. Nor do we need to understand previous theories of the sun as a god in Egyptian times to understand the process of fusion that occurs within it.

Conclusion. Top class. I like your academically cautious approach, with phrases such as 'although sometimes', 'in some circumstances' to give your conclusion a balanced and discerning character.

This essay scored a 12.0 in a mock BMAT exam.

Summary

- Medical school-specific examination results are highly correlated with good performance at medical school compared to other indicators.

- In the UKCAT examination, marks can be improved by practising questions.

- On-the-day performance is critical for high performance in the UKCAT.

- If you perform poorly in the examination, you may consider focusing your application on non-UKCAT medical schools.

- The BMAT is only used by Oxford, Cambridge and UCL.

- Section 1 is best prepared for by practice questions.

- The knowledge-base requirement for Section 2 is GCSE-level mathematics, chemistry, physics and biology, and should be diligently revised for.

- Poor marks in Section 3 are predictive of a poor performance at university, and such candidates will be selected against.

- Make use of the creativity framework to search your own knowledge base for relevant examples to support your arguments.

CHAPTER 7

The interview

How this chapter will help you get into medical school

The interview is the sternest test in the medical school admissions process, as academic ability, motivation for medicine and personal attributes can all be tested in one sitting. When I speak to admissions tutors, one of the recurrent themes is the high correlation between how much the tutor enjoyed the interview process and how successful the candidate was in being accepted to the medical school. What this means to you as the applicant is that you must learn to enjoy the interview and make the admissions tutors feel likewise.

This does not involve suddenly become a socially suave charmer of doctors. Preparing to be interesting is not simply a matter of being a good speaker, which is merely the presentation of your message. What makes someone interesting is the complete package, deep and broad knowledge of the subject on which they are speaking, together with interesting and sometimes non-standard viewpoints on certain topics. Also required are: organization skills, which allow you to put the information in an order that is natural and easy to follow; and finally the presentation, which is simply the icing on the cake.

In addition to these factors, specific question types can elicit other attributes. Science questions test for academic ability. Questions on motivation for medicine can be direct or involve using questions on knowledge of medicine and work experience. Personal attribute questions can involve extra-curricular activities and what you gained from them.

Integrating data from students, teaching experience and talking to admissions tutors from a variety of universities, I have created the model of dinner party theory for a logical, systems-based approach to increasing your storytelling ability.

Preparation

The interview is undoubtedly the most rigorous and demanding hurdle in the medical school admissions process. You must prepare meticulously, in all aspects of verbal and non-verbal communication skills. You will need a very solid knowledge base on the career and life of a doctor, and on current medical issues. You must practise interpreting and analysing ethical and legal scenarios. You will need to develop critical-thinking skills and an understanding (rather than simple knowledge) of a large body of scientific knowledge. Oxbridge interviews are so different that they may be considered a wholly new type of interview altogether, requiring familiarity with the principles of experimental design, data interpretation and scientific development.

In short, you will need to know and prepare far more than can be covered in a single chapter of a book. I recommend my companion book, *How to Succeed in Your Medical School Interview* (Kogan Page), which contains the vast amount of theoretical knowledge you will need to know, as well as over 200 questions and sample answers. It also details the true selection criteria based on discussions with interview panel members, and models of how to approach a question even if you do not know the answer. It also reveals patterns in the flow of interview questions, which can be modelled as 'chains', and methods to subtly manipulate the flow of these questions to your advantage. It tackles Oxbridge interviews as a completely separate entity, with practice questions and frameworks you can use to structure your answers.

Knowledge base

There are certain areas that you will need to very comfortable discussing. It is not enough to know the basics; what you should be aiming for is to be knowledgeable and interesting. This is because interview panel members consistently state that candidates whom they enjoy interviewing and find interesting are highly correlated with being given offers.

Here are some of the more common areas you should become familiar with:

- medicine:
    - life as a doctor;
    - life at medical school;
    - the GMC and its role; up-to-date examples of its actions;
    - the NHS and current issues;
    - health: definition;

- personal attributes:
    - strengths;
    - weaknesses;
    - stress: what causes it, what are the solutions for it;
    - teamwork;
    - leadership;
    - communication skills;
    - empathy;

- medical school:
    - the nature of the course itself: PBL, integrated or traditional;
    - extra-curricular activities and facilities;
    - hospitals associated with the institution;
    - areas of particularly distinguished research;

- ethics:
    - euthanasia;
    - consent;
    - confidentiality;
    - pro-life and pro-choice arguments concerning abortion;
    - the development of embryos, the minimum age of survival;

- law:
    - murder, manslaughter, suicide;
    - negligence;
    - data protection;
    - fertilization;

- current affairs:
    - HIV/AIDS;
    - swine flu;
    - genetic engineering/cloning;
    - assisted suicide.

Types of question

These fall under the categories of motivation for medicine, personal attributes, extra-curricular activities, law and ethics, medicine, and Oxbridge:

- Motivation for medicine:
    - Why do you want to study medicine?
    - Tell me about your work experience.
    - Tell me about your voluntary work.
    - Describe a day in the life of a doctor.
    - What appeals to you about hospital medicine?
    - What are the pros and cons of being a doctor?
    - Why have you chosen this medical school?
    - What is PBL?

- Personal attributes:
    - What are your two greatest strengths and weaknesses?
    - What is teamwork?
    - Tell me about a time when you demonstrated commitment.
    - Why is empathy important for a doctor?
    - What is leadership, and how do we know that you have leadership qualities?
    - Are communication skills natural or learned?

- Extra-curricular activities:
    - What will you contribute to the university?
    - What is your greatest achievement?
    - Tell us about your hobbies.
    - How do you cope with stress?

- Law and ethics:
  - What is the current law regarding euthanasia? What do you think of this?
  - A 14-year-old girl comes to your clinic asking for an abortion; what are the issues?
  - What is meant by 'medical futility'?
  - Why is consent for medical treatment so important? Under what circumstances does a patient lose the capacity to consent?
  - When is a doctor required to breach doctor–patient confidentiality?
  - 'First do no harm.' Is this statement still valid today?

- Medicine:
  - If you could donate £10 million to research one disease, which would it be and why?
  - What are the top three causes of death in the UK?
  - What is primary prevention of disease? Why is it so important?
  - What do you think of alternative or complementary medicine?
  - What is evidence-based medicine?

- Oxbridge:
  - How can we design an experiment to show which parts of the brain are involved in happiness?
  - Is hell exothermic or endothermic?
  - How many footballs can you fit into an aeroplane?
  - What data would we need to show that the BMI of Japanese migrants to America is affected by diet? Would this show that genetics are not involved in obesity?
  - What is a 'control' in an experiment and why is it important? How could we create a control group for a clinical trial involving acupuncture?

Again it is important to note that there are far too many possible questions to detail here, and you should actively seek other resources to help complete your knowledge for the interview process, via books and the internet. It is important to become familiar with the types of questions you will be asked, in order to minimize your nerves and have the appropriate material to reference in your answers.

How to become a great storyteller: the dinner party theory

Once you have acquired this background knowledge, it is important to consider how you are going to use it to give yourself the best chance of success. Dinner party theory (DPT) is a model I have developed specifically for medical school interviews, which was designed after consultation with admissions tutors from many universities, including Oxbridge, and draws on observations of social successes and failures in interacting with people.

If you consider a dinner party, where you sit down next to people you have never met before, what are the factors that make someone interesting to talk to?

Take the following examples:

Hi, I'm Ricky.

Hello, I'm Janine.

Nice to meet you. So what do you do?

Consider the following responses:

I'm a student.

I'm an English student.

I'm studying English literature, focusing on the works of Austen.

I'm studying English literature, focusing on the works of Austen, and I hope to pursue a career in journalism.

The first response is a simple statement of fact. The disadvantage is that the questioner will then have to prompt the speaker again to extract more data about what this actually involves. This makes the conversation feel like work, and several admissions tutors have stated that they dislike having to drag information and thought out of students.

The other responses are increasingly more interesting, and warrant follow-up questions. They add an element of personal touch, which is information relating to the person as opposed to the activity, and this is therefore individual to the person. In the final example it is the speaker's aspiration to work in a career in journalism. This response makes follow-up questioning far easier as it gives a number of cues to pick up on. It also gives the would-be journalist an advantage too, by directing the conversation to areas that they might be more comfortable talking about. It is also good micro-management, as the answer intrinsically generates interest, and the interviewer feels curious to find out more. How might we apply these observations to interview questions?

We can model the type of answers in a 'hierarchy of interest', going from the most bland to the most stimulating:

- list;

- explain;

- theory;

- manifest;

- reflect.

Imagine the following question: 'Tell me about your work experiences.'

The 'list' response would be: 'I did two weeks at hospital X, three weeks at hospital Y and another one-month placement in a lab.'

The lowest level of interest is generated by simple reporting. It is an absolute chore to mine further information from this candidate.

The 'explain' response would be: 'I've done attachments to a cardiology unit and an orthopaedics ward, and spent a month in a biochemistry laboratory.'

This is similar to listing but adds more detail, which adds a degree of interest and allows the interviewer to picture more of what went on. However, this would still require work on the part of the interviewer to interrogate you about the specific activities, which diminishes interest.

The 'theory' response would be: 'I've done attachments to a cardiology unit and an orthopaedics ward, and spent a month in a biochemistry laboratory. These work experiences have been a good way for me to learn about a career in medicine.'

This takes a step further in answering the question by linking the work experiences with the theory behind the question – which is, essentially, 'What do you know about medicine and how serious are you?' However, while it is informative, it is uninteresting and impersonal.

The 'manifest' response would be: 'I've done an attachment to a cardiology unit, where I followed the junior doctor to see what he does every day. I saw him examining patients, listening to their heart and lungs and then correlating his findings by looking at their X-rays, and I find this scientific investigation, coupled with doctor–patient interaction, a really appealing occupation.'

This begins by giving a more detailed account of specific events (eg examinations), ties it into some theory (scientific investigation) and then goes on to 'reflect' on how the student felt about it. This gives a stronger, more specific and more personalized answer to the question, which allows admissions tutors to be interested in the story, as well as noting your communication skills and organization.

In order to tell a good story, many factors are required. First, the material. There is a minimum amount of key knowledge that is a prerequisite to answering a question:

for example, 'Why do you want to become a doctor?' requires a knowledge of what the life of a doctor involves. However, the more you know about it, the richer your answer will potentially be. Most people know that being a doctor involves scientific knowledge and helping others.

DPT is most useful for questions that involve a degree of recounting events from your own life or describing yourself. These are mostly found in the medical and personal questions sections, although the principles of DPT can be applied to most questions.

Correct use of DPT involves a degree of preparation beyond that undertaken by most students for interview. It is important that you consider the potential questions and take time to explore all facets of the answers. For example, in addressing 'What makes you a good candidate for us?' it is important to consider what you will actually be doing at medical school, as well as what is involved in being a doctor. You could use the knowledge of the subjects taught at medical school in Chapter 2 to link with your own experiences to answer this question.

DPT framework

Here is the framework that I have constructed for answering questions using DPT:

1 Explain the theory.

2 Report the event.

3 Manifest an example.

4 Maintain interest with a unique perspective.

5 Reflect on how it made you feel.

6 Conclude.

Application of DPT

The fundamental principle of DPT is that when you answer a question, you make the answer interesting, relevant and intelligent. Answers will typically begin the explanation of theory, which can include definitions, and will move on to manifest examples, maintaining interest and reflecting upon the subject, with a clear-cut conclusion.

The maintaining interest section is the most important part of DPT. Admissions tutors admit that they sometimes get frustrated with the interview process as it produces 'a lot of the same answers from the same questions, which is frightfully dull'. As we established earlier, since having an interesting interview is the best correlate with successful application, this boredom is the exact situation we want to avoid. The question is how to avoid being the 15th person that day to give the same answers.

Let us consider what admissions tutors will already know about work experiences. They will already know that students are most likely to be observing rather than doing anything active. They will not know about the interesting patient whom you spoke to who ruptured his cruciate ligament, and for whom you felt most empathy as it ended his years of playing football. They will not know about the inspiring doctor whom you met, who had a wonderful attitude towards the patients that he treated, especially the confused patient with dementia who thought he was in a police station, and whom he managed to calm down and lead back to bed.

Consider the following question: 'What is your greatest achievement?'

Theory: 'I feel the most difficult things to achieve are long term.'

Manifest (factual): 'I would say my greatest is my black belt in karate. I trained for eight years at school.'

Maintain interest (descriptive): 'It was tough going having training after a long day at school, and at times it was physically very demanding – small things such as having bare feet in a wooden gym in the middle of winter! As you can imagine, it was tough going.' (Use gestures appropriately.)

The maintain interest section is the most important part of effective DPT. It gives a real, personal and unique spin on your answer, and will stimulate interest and empathy from your interview panel.

Reflect: 'I learned a great deal about discipline and commitment from persevering until I reached my goal of black belt, and I learned that achieving my goals by putting in effort and time is a rewarding and worthwhile activity. I hope to continue this pursuit in the future.'

Reflective learning is a key element of medical education and involves considering not only the event that you experienced but also how this affected you and how it will change what you do in the future.

Conclude: 'So I feel this is my most treasured achievement.' (slight nod)

The use of body language becomes important here, as the use of your hands, body and expression will help to signal to the interviewer when there is an 'interest-ing' section of your story. The most critical point is that there should be a change of atmosphere when you are at the maintain interest segment of the answer. This is achieved by the combination of content as well as non-verbal communication.

You can use phrases such as 'on balance', 'overall', 'finally', etc to indicate that you have come to the end of your answer. This maintains a smooth transition between question and answer, which allows more information exchange in a shorter time and enables you to score more highly than other candidates – providing that your answers are good ones!

DPT feedback

Just as a good comedian responds to their crowd, you too must be responsive to your audience, the interviewers. There is a time limit in which you have to execute your DPT routine in answer to a question, governed by the fact that interviews are finite events. If you exceed the time that you are allowed for a response, you will receive either direct or indirect cues from the interviewers to wrap up your story and move on. Indirect cues are predominantly given through body language, and some of the possible signs are listed below. A direct cue will be a verbal instruction to move on; ignore this at your peril.

Look for:

- eyes glazing over;

- fidgeting;

- reducing eye contact;

- sighing or coughing.

In the early stages of practising DPT, students have found that they either ramble on for too long when giving an answer or are too brief. It is vitally important that you practise your DPT skills on a daily basis in order to gain feedback. This can occur in speaking to peers, teachers, at parties, on the phone, or almost any situation where you are called upon to communicate. You can gauge the responses from your interviewers and readjust your timing and content to improve this response. Remember that doctors are scientists, and that by trying different formulations of the same information, you might get different results.

Learning tasks

Introduce yourself to someone new at a party, and ask them about what they like to do in their spare time. Assess how well their response uses DPT, and answer them back using it. Take heed of any indicators of disinterest.

Find a teacher you do not know particularly well, and ask them for five minutes of their time to discuss your career plans. Explain why you want to study medicine and answer any questions that may arise. Note down the teacher's non-verbal feedback as good or bad, and try to improve with the next teacher.

Summary

- The primary aim of dinner party theory is to make the interviewers enjoy the interview and find you interesting as a person. This is a key criterion for selection.

- The DPT framework for questions is most useful for medicine and personal attribute-type questions.

- It involves the following steps:

  - theory;
  - manifesting example;
  - maintain interest;
  - reflection;
  - conclusion.

- Avoid remaining solely on the theoretical plane for medicine and personal attribute-type questions.

- Use anecdotes that are tried and tested to be interesting.

- Always be alert for direct and indirect feedback and respond accordingly.

- Reflect on what you have learned.

- Conclude strongly.

Practical considerations

The interview itself

The interview will involve facing a panel made up of doctors, faculty staff and medical students. They are aiming to select the best candidates for places at their medical school. Bear in mind that some of the attributes – such as academic ability – have already been assessed to a great degree in your UCAS form and, if applicable, medical school admissions results. Qualities that are more difficult to assess on paper, such as motivation for medicine, and personal attributes, will be the focus of the event.

You will have already seen the types of questions that come up. You will have prepared by reading around the issues, constructing answers and discovering your own opinions about certain subjects. It is important to be confident and well spoken in the interview. If you have problems with being heard, make sure you practise speaking up. A patient may become impatient if they have to ask you to repeat every other sentence; and the interview panel will be the same.

The first interview is always the most difficult, and students often report that they get into the flow of interviews after their first. Nerves are expected, and acceptable, and admissions tutors state that the content and organization of the answers are the key elements; the delivery is of less importance than these factors.

For further details on how to manage the interview panel, the direction of the interview, questions to which you do not know the answer and nasty interviewers, see my companion book, *How to Succeed in Your Medical School Interview* (Kogan Page).

Appearance

The dress code for interview is formal. For men this means suit and tie in conservative colours, smart and polished shoes, tidy appearance and no unnatural hair colours. For women it means a suit or skirt in similarly conservative hues, with moderate make-up and accessories. This is not specified by all universities, but when applying for a course that leads to professional career, it helps the admissions tutor to extrapolate how you might choose to present yourself in the future.

Arrive early and give yourself plenty of time for unexpected delays.

The night before the interview

If you are applying to a university in another city, you will most probably be staying overnight. Make sure you have left enough time for travel between locations.

Do not try to learn new material. There is a vast amount of material that you will have covered in your preparations up to this point, and the most useful thing you can do is consolidate. Information will either be 'interview ready' – data that you know well, and more than just the bare bones – or not. Moreover, it is important that you are comfortable verbalizing and discussing the material, and this comes about by a combination of input (reading, research) as well as practising output (mock interviews, practice with friends, talking about it in front of a mirror). Any new information you acquire in the final couple of days will not be retained at such a high quality and therefore should be avoided. Instead, try to focus on reinforcing your existing knowledge, and include the practice of verbalizing (saying out loud) key points and difficult words to enhance the 'output' element of your communication skills.

Relaxation. It is very important that your mind is fresh and enthusiastic for the challenge ahead. Just as an actor who practises a scene too many times might find it hard to look surprised when a murderer appears from around the curtain for the 30th time, you might lose the will to discuss your love of science if it's been going through your head too often the night before the exam. You will therefore need an activity that can genuinely take your mind off things for a significant period.

Revision. Construct revision sheets to refresh yourself on key definitions and terms; also note down the anecdotes that you can draw upon for medicine, personal attribute and work experience questions.

Biology. Experiment with your meals and find the type of food that you can eat without it making you feel sleepy. Once you have established what this is, try to have the same or similar products available for the day of interview itself so that you will be able to focus for the duration of the interview. For many people, fat-rich foods such as fish and chips cause bloating and wind – which are not ideal. Sugary foods often give a 'high' as serum glucose levels peak, but then give a rebound 'low' as increasing insulin levels drive the glucose into the cells, leaving you feeling shaky and weak. Caffeine can lead to an over-aroused state in which you appear more nervous, and may also heighten feelings of anxiety. However, all of the above are just guidelines, the bottom line being that people respond variably to different foods and it is important to establish your own personal optimal nutrition in the peri-interview period. You may also find these data useful around exam periods. It would be a shame for a future doctor to give a poor performance because of lack of knowledge of nutritional metabolism, both theoretical and applied!

The morning of the interview

When you wake up, just remember that if you've been working through the exercises, questions and learning tasks in this book, you will be better prepared than most candidates. Be reassured that there are many people who think that it is not possible to prepare for an interview, and you will be in a good position. The last thing to remember is that you are applying for a long course at university and working life after that, and that you should be genuinely looking forward to it as a wonderful, rich and exciting experience, culminating in a challenging and rewarding career.

Some key points:

- Do some active relaxation to take your mind off the interview.

- Get a good night's sleep.

- Eat well and correctly.

- Remember to apply the basic principles of DPT and chain navigation.

- Look forward to your future in medicine, and be genuinely excited!

Summary

- The interview is the most challenging stage of the medical school admissions process.

- The types of question fall into the categories of: motivation for medicine, personal attribute, science, ethics and law.

- Do not underestimate the huge amount of preparation required to give a confident and fluent performance at interview. All the information you will need to succeed in the interview cannot be given in a single chapter of a book.

- Knowledge of the relevant facts is necessary but not sufficient.

- Good delivery of information is a technical skill that can be learned and practised.

- One of the main selection criteria is the interviewer's enjoyment and interest.

- Interest can be generated and maintained by using DPT techniques.

- Dress code is formal.

- Have your anecdotes and study material written down, and go over them the night before the interview.

- On the day of the interview, be genuinely excited about wanting to start a career in medicine, and let the interview panel see it.

CHAPTER 8

International and graduate students

How this chapter will help you get into medical school

There are several considerations which the international applicant must make in addition to the ones made by home students. First, is a medical course in the UK the one you really wish to undertake? This chapter will help you weigh up the benefits of studying in the UK rather than at a local university in your home country or one in another country. Second, will you adapt to studying in a foreign country, in a language that may not be your first? Will you be able to cope with the different environment? This chapter will suggest some ways to demonstrate that you have considered this, as well as actively investigated and taken steps towards mitigating this disadvantage.

The graduate student will have to distinguish themselves further from an already distinguished crowd. Academic considerations go beyond that of simply your degree class, and extra-curricular activities must expand in scope to facilitate this. Employment may be considered as a tool in your application.

Procedure

It is important to state that there are many differences between the international admissions policies of various countries, as well as those of institutions; these are too numerous to be described in detail in this chapter. These policies are also subject to change from time to time. Your school, the university prospectuses and admissions offices will have up-to-date technical information on applications procedures.

Some universities will send an admissions tutor out to the respective country to interview. This is usually just one person rather than a full panel as you might expect in interviews based in the UK.

However, the principles of a successful international application are still applicable to the process.

Several admissions tutors state that international applicants have to satisfy their criteria for academic ability and personal attributes in the same way as for home students. However, you will be competing against other international students for a fixed number of places at each medical school. It might help to think of this as applying to the international 'section' of a university in terms of competitiveness, with limited numbers and tough competition.

Scholarships

Some national governments offer scholarships to students to fund their medical studies. These are often phenomenally competitive, and successful scholarship recipients are usually high achievers in their chosen extra-curricular activities as well. Scholarships may also come with conditions for service or return to the home country to work, although this varies by nation. Enquire via schoolteachers, universities or directly to the relevant government department (usually the ministry of education or health).

English

In order to study any subject in the UK you will need a good standard of English, to cope with the taught material as well as living in general. However, in medicine this is even more important, as you will be interacting with patients, possibly very early on in the course and certainly in the course of your clinical training. You will need to be equipped to listen to medical histories, explain diagnoses and treatments and deal with the plethora of different accents and colloquialisms in various parts of the UK. You will also need to write medical notes and communicate efficiently with colleagues.

It is therefore import to focus on improving your communication skills in English. You do not have to speak the Queen's English in terms of accent, although you will have to be comprehensible. The important thing is having a solid and wide command of vocabulary so that your comprehension is good. It will also allow you to formulate correct and succinct responses to questions at interview, and write a fluent personal statement. Focusing on the fundamentals of language is far more important than cosmetic accent changing.

'The humour of lecturers took a lot of getting used to! I found it hard to tell if they were being serious or joking, and I would often have to ask a colleague. I got used to the British humour quite quickly and now I love listening out for their sarcastic comments.'

UK vs the rest of the world

Questions you should consider:

Do you know about the NHS?
It is important that you are able to compare and contrast this with your home country's medical system. Is there more of a focus on private healthcare? What provision is there for the healthcare of the impoverished? What are the benefits of your country's healthcare system over the NHS? In what ways is the NHS superior?

Do you have an idea of your long-term goals?
Would you wish to return to your home country to work? If so, be prepared for questions such as 'Why should we invest our time training you when you will just go back home to practise afterwards?' It may be useful to note that the UK government spends quite a substantial amount of money on international aid, so it approves of the principle of helping countries in need. As an international student, your fees may not be subsidized, so you will be bringing revenue to the university. You will also spend money in the UK, stimulating the economy, and you will be paying tax, all of which contribute to offsetting any losses. You may be bringing back valuable skills to a community that has a great need for them. You will also be bringing a different perspective and spreading cultural awareness and insight when you return home.

Are you considering staying in the UK to work?

Make sure you know the career structure for doctors in the UK well, as described in Chapter 1. This is important to demonstrate that you are not simply considering the theory of working overseas, but that you also have the investigative nature to seek firm answers. It is helpful if you have been to visit the UK as it will enable you to draw upon some experiences.

Have you considered local universities in your home country?

There are some important differences between studying in the UK and studying in your home country. First, there is the learning environment, which will be English. It may be easier to study in your mother tongue, and when you graduate you may need to relearn medical terminology in another language if you choose to work in another country.

There are also some important technical differences when you have graduated. In Hong Kong, for example, local graduates can begin working for the hospital authority immediately. There is only one year of internship or housemanship, compared with two in the UK. This is not subject to the European Working Directive, so the working hours and on-call rota are significantly more demanding on doctors than in the UK. At the time of writing, hospitals can operate a one-in-three rota for on-call at night, meaning that you will work a full day, be on call at night and work a half day the following day, all without a break from being in hospital. This gives the advantages of being able to discuss the patients you have treated overnight with the day team at the time of handover, and of having a greater amount of experience and training in a shorter time. Its disadvantages include increased stress among junior doctors and also a potential danger to patients medicated by very tired doctors.

If you graduate from the UK and wish to work in Hong Kong, you must pass a licensing exam that is particularly difficult and has a pass rate of around 5–12 per cent. You may take this examination only after one year of work experience, and if you are successful, whatever level you are at in the UK, you will have to undertake the year of internship before starting training.

Therefore if you are choosing to come to the UK, this may impact your future career.

Community support

Within each university there is usually an informal support network for helping students settle in, and this may be particularly useful for international students in helping you adjust to your new environment. If you have seniors from your school who are studying in the UK, get in touch and ask them for advice as early as possible. Many current international students have described how there is a strong feeling of support from school alumni because they have experienced the difficulty of the transition themselves. They may be the best source of support for advice or practical tips for living in the UK. Issues ranging from clothing, items to bring, personal safety and travel may all be consulted.

Many university student unions operate a 'parent' system in which a pair of current students look after their 'children', who would be new students to the university, and help them settle in to day-to-day life. Universities may also have an international students union which may offer services varying from giving information to meeting incoming students at train stations as they come to the university.

It is important to be aware of such measures as they may be useful in answering questions regarding how you will cope in a foreign country.

Are you really independent?

The second element of demonstrating your ability to cope with a challenging environment is to draw upon experiences you have had during your school time. It is important to impress upon the admissions tutors that you can manage under periods of duress, difficult conditions or reduced support.

'In my time undertaking national service with the Singapore army, I was thrust into a new environment, strange accommodation and many new things to learn. I like to think that I thrive on challenges, and I became friends with new acquaintances whose support helped me to get through. I went on to be promoted to second lieutenant and I feel that this experience has honed my coping mechanisms, while leaving me eager for my next trial.'

How will you be making a contribution to the university?

This is a common interview question for both home and international students. However, I have had a word of warning from an admissions tutor about students who are too focused on cultural contributions, to the detriment of mentioning other ways to contribute. He states that sometimes international interviewees sound so focused on being an ambassador of their country that they don't seem to want to integrate or try new things. For example, one student said he was going to be involved in his nation's traditional dance, get involved in cultural nights and even feed hungry neighbours traditional foods. While this was all very admirable, it gave the impression of being a little one-dimensional. A better approach is to integrate your own interests, your cultural interests and potential new interests in order to give a more balanced impression. This applies to both the personal statement and interview.

Personal statement

The main principles of writing the personal statement remain unchanged from a normal application. Use the different nature of medical schools to choose an integrated, traditional or PBL-type statement. One additional characteristic that is important for success is independence, as we have discussed above, and it is helpful to include an example of how you can best demonstrate this.

Given the word-limit constraint, it is often better to remember that you are applying to a medical school rather than a country, and not put too much focus on the 'international' aspect of your statement. If you wish to include statements about applying to the UK, incorporate a prospective and enthusiastic statement such as:

> *I am excited and ready to take on the challenge of studying medicine in the UK – excelling in a world-class, cosmopolitan and competitive medical school.*

This must be backed up by evidence of your independence, academic ability and commitment, as described previously.

If you have school alumni who are studying in the UK, they can be helpful in checking over your statement. It is important not to make grammatical errors as this would reflect poorly on your language skills.

Graduate students

There are now many graduate courses for medicine, which require applicants to undertake an undergraduate degree. Their features include:

- Courses are condensed – typically four years in length;

- High intensity – because of this compression, the learning curve is steeper and the time you will have to assimilate information is less;

● Competitive – a high applicant-to-place ratio, which means a high overall quality of applicant.

Alternative route

If you have applied to medicine but have been unsuccessful, you could undertake an 'enforced' gap year as discussed in Chapter 3. However, an alternative route is to take another degree and progress to take medicine as a graduate course. This is a good choice, particularly if you are not keen to take a gap year, and it will keep you in an academic environment while you pursue your goal. It also may open up the opportunity for alternative careers once you have had some university experience, which you may not have considered before.

However you should note that, if this is your plan, there are several steps you should consider if you wish to maximize your chances for admission. These are listed below.

Academics

There is a higher selection pressure on graduate courses, owing to the large number and high quality of candidates for fewer places. In Chapter 3 it was noted that buyer's remorse gives rise to academic ability being the most reliable of the three indicators of a candidate's ability to study medicine. This is even more true of graduates, as school applicants with A levels correlate well with performance at medical school, but university grades correlate even better with performance at a further university course.

It is absolutely vital to perform well in your degree. The minimum level of degree required is 2.1. However, given the fierce competition, it is important to distinguish yourself from others as much as possible.

Other than achieving as highly as possible in your degree, earning prizes and distinctions will help. Once you enter university, read faculty websites for any competitions that you might be able to participate in, such as essay-writing competitions or research.

Publications will also be a distinguishing achievement, and if you can manage to get original work published in a peer-reviewed national or international journal, or even a student journal, this will certainly count in your favour. If you are undertaking a science-based degree, there may be a research element involved as part of the course. If this is not the case, check within your department to see if research opportunities are available.

Extra-curricular activities

A three-year undergraduate degree, particularly with long summer breaks, gives you plenty of time to supplement your application with experiences and activities demonstrating the personal attributes required for medicine.

In particular, it gives you a chance to commit to a long-term undertaking of your choice. This can be easier to implement than at school as you have a more flexible timetable at university. Some more original candidates have even undertaken activities such as becoming a special constable with the police, and doing volunteer patrols. Such activities will demonstrate your maturity, ability to handle responsibility and commitment, as well as showing an interest in public service. One candidate undertook training to undertake a marathon in the Sahara desert as a fund-raising event, which again is something beyond the ability of most school-aged candidates, and demonstrates perseverance.

Employment

There is a subgroup of applicants who do not plan to take an undergraduate degree with a view to studying medicine, but come to the idea at some point during their career and decide to apply for graduate medical school. If this is the case with you, you will have to demonstrate all the attributes and genuine, long-standing nature of your investigation into medicine as a career in the same way as other candidates.

Employment is a useful way of showing that you can handle professional commitments and lead a responsible working life. It should be considered if there is a field of work that interests you, as admissions tutors prefer candidates who have had more life experience in general and still wish to pursue medicine; they are seen as more reliable. However, this does not preclude entry immediately after graduating from your first degree, particularly if you have a strong academic track record and an impressive extra-curricular profile.

Summary

- International students face high levels of competition.

- English is a vital skill, and focus should be on improving comprehension and vocabulary.

- Ask yourself the key questions, including background knowledge and long-term goals.

- Personal statements should be focused on applying to the medical school rather than the country or system.

- This means that most of the principles of the personal statement are the same as for home students.

- However, it is important to demonstrate independence, with examples where possible.

- Graduate courses are four years in length, and are intense and competitive.

- If you intend to apply, you should focus on achieving very highly in academics.

- Prizes, scholarships, awards and publications should be pursued as much as possible.

- Extra-curricular activities that demonstrate maturity and long-term commitment can help distinguish you from other candidates.

- This includes employment.

CHAPTER 9

Further resources

The recommended reading list is not a syllabus of books to power through before interview, it is a library to be dipped into for your enjoyment and expansion of the mind, and will help you in a much more diffuse way that simply saying 'I read this book.' I have included recommended films and other media because these are increasingly becoming the media in which important issues are discussed and information conveyed.

Reading list

General medical and scientific knowledge:

- *The Selfish Gene* by Richard Dawkins; Oxford University Press, 1976

- *The Man Who Mistook His Wife for a Hat* by Oliver Sacks; Summit Books, 1985

- *On Call: A Doctor's Days and Nights in Residency* by Emily Transue; St Martin's Griffin, 2005

- *Bioethics: an Anthology* by Helga Kuhse and Peter Singer; Blackwell, 2006

- *An Introduction to Medical Law* by Peter Blondel Marquand; Butterworth-Heinemann, 2000

- *Psychology and Sociology Applied to Medicine* by Beth Alder *et al*; 3rd edn, Churchill Livingstone, 2009

Movies

- *12 Angry Men*. The definitive method of how to construct academically cautious reasoned argument.

- *21*. A great example of DPT in action in a medical school application. Also, look out for applied statistics.

- *Patch Adams*. A motivation film, with a focus on 'softer' skills, including empathy and communication skills. A must-watch for PBL medical school applicants.

- *Philadelphia*. A deep look into the stigma attached to diseases, in this case HIV.

- *One Flew over the Cuckoo's Nest*. A tale of an inmate's stay on a psychiatric ward, and the human qualities of hope and enthusiasm.

TV series

- *House, M.D.* In equal parts intriguing and entertaining, this series is definitely worth a watch.

- *Scrubs*. Take with a very large pinch of salt. Hospital life does not really resemble this, but it is light-hearted entertainment with a medical twist.

- *Grey's Anatomy*.

- *ER*.

The internet

- Médecins Sans Frontières: http://www.msf.org.uk/;

- International Committee of the Red Cross: http://www.icrc.org/.

Candidates often mention a desire to work in international aid organizations as one of their motivations for undertaking medicine. Make sure you know about how they work, their aims and how you might contribute to them in the future.

- TED talks: www.ted.com/talks

This is an annual conference entitled 'Technology, Entertainment and Design – Ideas Worth Sharing', comprising a series of lectures by some of the world's greatest thinkers on subjects as varied as science, economics, statistics and sociology. Lectures are only 18 minutes long and presented in an engaging and entertaining manner. There is an entire section dedicated to innovation in medicine, entitled 'Medicine without Borders'. Here are some recommended lectures:

- 'Your health depends on where you live: introducing the concept of geomedicine': Bill Davenhall.
- 'Surgery's past, present and robotic future': Catherine Mohr.
- 'How statistics fool juries': Peter Donnelly.

Videos

- Sir Terry Pratchett's Dimbleby Lecture: 'Shaking hands with death'.

Oxbridge interview preparation

For Oxbridge (it is recommended that you try to borrow these books from your library, as they are very expensive and long. Do not try to read them cover to cover; instead, try reading one or two chapters that interest you, and tie in their knowledge with your existing knowledge in biology, chemistry and other disciplines):

- *Textbook of Medical Physiology* by Arthur C Guyton and John E Hall; 11th edn, Saunders, 2005
- *Clinical Anatomy* by Richard S Snell; 7th edn, Lippincott Williams and Wilkins, 2003
- *Neurophysiology* by Roger Carpenter; 4th edn, Hodder Arnold, 2002
- *Biochemistry for Dummies* by John T Moor and Richard H Langley; John Wiley and Sons, 2008
- *Rang and Dale's Pharmacology* by Humphrey Rang and Maureen Dale; 6th edn, Churchill Livingstone
- *Kumar and Clark's Clinical Medicine* by Parveen Kumar and Michael L Clark; 7th edn, Saunders

Other reading

The following books may be outside the direct medical field but relate to experimental design, use of data or scientific interpretation:

- *The Tipping Point: How little things can make a big difference* by Malcolm Gladwell; Abacus, 2001

- *The Greatest Show on Earth: The evidence for evolution* by Richard Dawkins; Bantam Press, 2009

- *Freakonomics* by Steven Levitt and Stephen J Dubner; William Morrow, 2005

Forums

www.newmediamedicine.com and other forums for students can be immensely useful, and allow you to post questions and share information anonymously. Be cautious with the advice given, however, as it is often unmoderated and can range from unsure advice to pure speculation. The other thing to avoid is any panic induced by what you hear on the forums; anonymity can allow for boasting and exaggeration – don't let this affect you negatively. Furthermore, don't be tempted to simply follow what you see as a 'winning formula'; use the principles that have been discussed throughout this book and remember that you are crafting your own personalized application.

Facebook

This is the most popular social networking website at the time of writing, and is an excellent way of sharing photos, news and events with friends around the globe. However, it is also an easy way to vet candidates and their appropriateness for a place at medical school followed by a career as a doctor. There have been reports of admissions tutors checking Facebook profiles before interviewing candidates, and in some cases pictures or comments have affected the candidates' chances negatively. In the run-up to admissions, make sure the privacy settings on your profile are set so that only your friends can access your account. It is also recommended that you spring-clean your profile in case access may be gained. In particular, any compromising photographs, comments about teachers, etc should be strictly removed as they may be viewed very dimly.

Medical admissions courses

Medsim is a course designed for would-be medical school applicants to help familiarize them through practical courses and lectures. It is held in Nottingham University and is helpful both in content and allowing potential students to meet peers and discuss the applications process.

Medical applications tutors

Speaking as a tutor myself, there are a large number of activities which can aid a student in their bid to win a place at medical school. The best tutors will pick up on the individual interests of a student and help to develop these as they prepare to apply to medical school. They will give balanced advice about a career in medicine and about medical schools. They will talk about interesting current affairs in medicine and science, as well as discussing ethical and legal problems in an appealing manner. Tutors advise on generic reading, scientific discussion or about the career of medicine as a whole. Tutors may also be able to perform mock interviews, which are helpful in putting the interview theory into practice under pressured conditions. I use a video analysis technique which allows the student to look back on their own performance and pick out the key learning points. It also allows them to keep a catalogue of progress and see their improvement over time.

For Oxbridge applications, tutors might focus more on engaging scientific problems and questions, which will help maintain and develop a genuine curiosity for science, which is one of the key criteria for acceptance.

The best judges of the value of a tutor are the students themselves, as they will complain about dull and unoriginal teaching methods. They will also be more excited about medicine and medical school if the tutor is doing their job well. Do not hesitate to shop around until you find a tutor who truly stimulates you in the field of medicine. You can find tutors on websites such as www.tutors4me.co.uk or www.bluetutors.co.uk.

CHAPTER 10

Fees and funding

How this chapter will help you get into medical school

The previous chapters have detailed the long process of how to win a place at medical school. This chapter enables you to plan practically for the costs ahead by detailing apparent and hidden costs, as well as sources of funding and relief.

The cost of medical school

There are several considerations to make in regard to finances. Medical school is more expensive than most other courses by sheer virtue of its length. As discussed in Chapter 2, if you are considering taking a six-year course or a course where you could take an intercalated degree, cost may come into your decision-making process.

Fees

In 2009 the annual fees for medical school per year were £3,145.

For home (UK) students, an NHS bursary is available to pay for the fees for the final year of study.

For international students, fees vary from institution to institution but are substantially more than for home and EU students. They also increase at stages in the course, and can be between £11,000 and £16,000 for the first two years, and for the last three years increase to between £19,000 and £25,000.

Additional costs

There are some additional costs which can arise by virtue of the differences between medicine and other courses. First, there are costs and equipment related to study. In order to examine patients, you will need to purchase a stethoscope, which range in price from £40 to £140 depending on quality. It may be useful to have your own opthalmoscope, a piece of optical equipment for examining the eye, which can be up to £175 for a model appropriate for a student.

Medical books can be expensive, and although you will be able to find most of them in the university library, when all the medical students on a course are looking for the same book, this can make things difficult. There are revision courses for medical finals run by the MDU (Medical Defence Union) and the MPS (Medical Protection Society), which can cost around £120 per day, to help you consolidate your knowledge before examinations. Likewise, there are databanks of online questions to practise for finals, which charge a subscription fee.

Transport costs can mount up, especially in the later clinical years. This is because most universities have more students than they can train in a central hospital, and therefore dispatch students to placement in district general hospitals, which can be in other towns. For example, at Cambridge University, central training takes place in Addenbrooke's Hospital in Cambridge, but students will undertake placements of four to eight weeks weeks as far afield as Ipswich, Peterborough or Luton.

Accommodation may or may not be provided free of charge by the university during these attachments, and this varies by institution. This is usually in the doctors' accommodation of the hospital if it is available. Furthermore, gaining experience in other specialties such as general practice, which do not have such on-site accommodation, may necessitate a daily commute.

With all this travel, a car is often useful for access and convenience, with all the associated costs.

Overall, the British Medical Association Annual Report for 2009 gives the following figures for medical students in their final year of studies:

- Average level of debt: £22,821.

- Average cost per month of accommodation: £361.

Sources of funding

Student grants

These are means-tested grants awarded by your local education authority (LEA) after an assessment of your household income, to support you at medical school. Details are available from your LEA.

Student loans

These are low-interest loans provided to home students by the Student Loans Company. Repayment of student loans is tied to your earnings, and once you earn above a certain threshold you will slowly repay your loan as a percentage of your salary. Many students can fund their costs of living through these loans.

NHS bursaries

These are non-repayable bursaries to assist home students in medical school, and cover the cost of tuition for the last year for almost all students. There is a means-tested element for additional support. Further details at www.nhsstudent-grants.co.uk.

Scholarships

Universities can offer scholarships to excellent candidates, which will cover the cost of tuition fees and sometimes make a contribution towards living costs or accommodation. These are merit based and can involve writing an essay or attending an additional interview after shortlisting for a scholarship. It is well worth enquiring at each university, as winning a scholarship will also be a notable achievement later on in your career.

The armed forces offer cadetships with paid tuition and substantial financial stipends. These are offered on the basis of a return on service, normally about six years, in, for example, the Royal Army Medical Corps (RAMC) as part of the conditions. Contact the armed forces for details.

Summary

- Medical school is a long and expensive training.

- There is a large average debt on leaving medical school.

- Help is available for applicants from lower-income backgrounds.

- Scholarships are offered at many universities and offer both financial support and prestige.

Appendix

Templates for interview preparation activities

These templates are designed to summarize your key information. They should be used after your medical interview preparation activities such as work experience, voluntary work or additional reading. Each of them should only take five to ten minutes to complete, and they will form an invaluable resource when you become time pressured as the interview approaches. They will help you reflect on what you have learned from each stage of your experience and be better able to link this to your future studies in medicine and practice as a doctor.

Most students will have undertaken work experience, but they may have trouble recalling specific incidences. Try to maintain a folder of entries, and update it regularly. You don't have to complete a template each and every time you finish reading an article or news story, but do it for important or memorable ones.

Use the templates as a basis to refresh yourself on key facts and events you will talk about at interview.

Use the information to design DPT-based (dinner party theory defined on page 86) answers for questions.

Download the templates from: www.koganpage.com/HowToGetIntoMedicalSchool using the password: MED5649

WORK EXPERIENCE DIARY TEMPLATE

Attachment and date

Cardiology team, Lewisham Hospital

What did you learn from the day?

I was attached to the cardiology team, and followed them as they did the ward round and visited patients. I was shown a few ECGs, and it was explained to me that they are electrocardiograms, which are made by placing electrodes around the heart and measuring the electric current that is generated when the heart contracts. This can show if there are problems in conducting the electricity.

How did this affect you?

I quite enjoyed seeing how the biology of muscle contraction is applied in the everyday work of doctors in investigating patients. I began to see how my study of sciences will be important in my future career.

Any personal attributes witnessed in doctors or other members of staff?

Communication skills. The doctor I was following was the senior house officer, who was explaining his findings to a patient with chest pain. It was quite interesting to see how he reassured her that although she had a heart condition called angina (when you get heart pain from insufficient blood supply to the heart), this was quite different from having a heart attack as the damage was not permanent and heart tissue would not have died as a result.

He explained later that he wrote 'MI' in the notes – standing for myocardial infarction – but advised me to avoid using medical jargon when talking to patients where possible as it can be distracting and confusing.

Additional notes

In interviews, and even in designing your personal statement, the personal attributes of communication skills, teamwork, leadership, empathy and commitment will come up repeatedly. Use this section to think about why these characteristics are important, and how doctors you have met display them – or in some cases fail to display them. You will be better able to refer to these experiences once they are recorded.

SCIENTIFIC OR MEDICAL ARTICLE TEMPLATE

Title of article

Acupuncture pain molecule pinpointed

Date and source of article

BBC Health, 30 May 2010

Summarized contents (three sentences max)

Scientists may have found the molecule that is responsible for the effect of pain relief in acupuncture.
In experiments with mice, an increased level of adenosine has been found around the needle area.
Adenosine is a neuro-transmitter involved in pain pathways.

The reasons for having a three-sentence summary are to have an efficient way of presenting the article to an interview panel without either being too brief or too wordy – what you will want to try to do is move into discussion of the article rather than simply reporting it, and this is best done by succinct expression of the article's key concepts.

Why did you find this article interesting?

Acupuncture and alternative therapies are popular, but I wonder whether or not they are effective. It seems that acupuncture has the strongest evidence base, from the information that I have read, but it is still viewed quite sceptically by many people. One of the reasons medical pharmacology is often more accepted than acupuncture is that there is often a well-characterized mechanism of action, and it is therefore interesting to see that they have found a possible mechanism for the effect that acupuncture has.

Remember to use academic caution in your answers – articles may claim more than they can reasonably do – so words such as 'possible', 'indicates, 'suggests' are often more useful than 'proves' or 'demonstrates'.

Additional reading to be done in this area

    The placebo effect
    Adenosine
    Pain relief medication
    Other alternative therapies

If you are going to bring up a topic, it is wise to know more than is in a single article – for example, know more about pain control medications, so that you can give a rounded answer – and follow up on any further questions.

UNIVERSITY OPEN DAY TEMPLATE

University attended and date

Initial impressions

What impresses you about the course, facilities and location?

Information from students spoken to

This can be a useful area in which to document 'insider' information, including what the course was like, and the pros and cons from current students' perspectives.

Final impression

It can be useful to see if your impressions have changed after you have left the university at the end of your visit. Can you envisage yourself studying at this institution for many years? Do you like the town and environment?

Questions for interview

Any particular issues which you felt have not been answered by the prospectus and open day, or any areas which you find particularly interesting, eg research fields, famous graduates?

RECOMMENDED READING

Title of book or other reading material

This can be a book or other material that might be interesting for interview – you will also find this documentation useful for general discussion.

Summary of contents (three sentences max)

Again, have a brief summary of the book or other reading material; this will allow you to move into discussion.

Interesting themes of the book or other material

Why did this book or other material appeal to you? Can you characterize the themes that were challenging or interesting? What are the issues involved?

Particular stories or sections of interest

It can be useful to reference particular events, chapters or characters of the book – not least because your interviewers might be testing whether or not you have in fact read it! This section can be used to refresh your memory just prior to the interview, so that you can use these examples to highlight your points in discussion.

Personal reflection

How did it affect you, what came up from the book or other reading material that you could empathize with?

APPLICATION FOR MEDICAL WORK EXPERIENCE, SAMPLE LETTER

Your name
Address and postcode

Name of individual you are contacting
Name of medical institution
Address and postcode

Date

Dear *(title and name of addressee)*

My name is Joseph Bloggs. I am a student studying for my AS levels at the Joe Blog Academy for Gifted Children. I would like to apply for a work experience placement at your hospital/department for the week of 16–20 July.

I will be applying for a place in medical school this coming autumn, and I am currently studying biology, chemistry, physics and English literature at AS level. I would love to gain some experience of the hospital environment, and see medical staff working with patients, so that I can further my aim of becoming a doctor.

I have previously undertaken a voluntary work placement at the Castleford Residential Home, where I helped out with day-to-day tasks and spoke to the residents about their experiences. I also currently attend a weekly programme run by my school for reading to the blind, called the 60+ Scheme.

Please find my CV attached. If you would like a reference, I would be happy to supply you with the contact details for my form tutor or head of year.

I look forward to hearing from you.

Yours sincerely

(signature)

Joseph Bloggs

ADDITIONAL SAMPLE BMAT ESSAY 1

'The attainment of scientific knowledge has been effected, to a great extent, by the help of scientific errors.' Discuss.

Many scientific errors and accidental discoveries have led to a greater attainment of scientific knowledge. There have been countless accidental discoveries, from normal everyday objects like Coke, Post-its and plastic, to everyday essentials like saccharin and smart dust (which monitors the water filtering system), and to medicinal discoveries such as penicillin, Viagra and the pacemaker. I will be looking at some famous examples of accidental discoveries, including penicillin, the pacemaker and radioactivity.

Penicillin has been one of the most widely used antibiotics ever since Sir Alexander Fleming discovered it in 1928. He went away on holiday and forgot to clear his agar plates, and when he came back he observed that the colonies of the bacterium *Staphylococcus aureua* could be destroyed by the mould *Penicillium notatum* that grows naturally on fruit, proving that there was an antibacterial agent there. However, afterwards, Fleming couldn't culture penicillin and the project was abandoned until the 1940s during the Second World War, when Howard Florey and Ernst Chain isolated the active ingredient and developed an antibiotic that was used to help soldiers who had bacterial infections from their injuries in the war.

The pacemaker came about when an American engineer called Wilson Greatbatch was working on a circuit that could help record fast heart sounds. He reached into the box for the resistor to complete the circuit and pulled out the wrong circuit part. Then the circuit pulsed in the same beat as the human heartbeat. Later, this was developed into a portable pacemaker that could be implanted into the human body and later actually into the heart.

Radioactivity was unknown until an accidental discovery when Henri Becquerel was using natural fluorescent minerals to study the properties of X-rays. When he exposed them to sunlight and then placed them on photographic plates wrapped in black paper, with a key on top, there was later a strong and clear image of the key on the photographic plates. He tested the effect further with the famous image of his wife's hand with her wedding ring.

However, accidental discoveries and scientific errors do not always end up making amazing drugs or products. Most things need to be tested thoroughly and examined and rechecked before allowing that knowledge to be made fact. For example, many people thought that thalidomide was a fantastic discovery and helped to get rid of morning sickness in pregnant women. But a few months later, when the babies of mothers who had taken thalidomide were born deformed, researchers realized that they hadn't tested the drug on pregnant animals. Nowadays, having banned the drug from the stores, the pharmaceutical companies are researching the other effects of thalidomide on diseases and have found it to have an effect on leprosy.

A drug that was discovered accidentally is LSD, which was discovered in 1943 when Swiss chemist Albert Hofmann touched a chemical he was researching to induce childbirth and experienced the first acid hit. Since then, LSD has been used as a recreational drug, although it is harmful to the users and has been known to kill hundreds of users per year.

In conclusion, I think that scientific attainment has been affected to a great extent by scientific errors – even unsuccessful errors, as scientists have then gone back and checked over what had gone wrong and how it could be readjusted to make it right. The big scientific discoveries have been found through accidental discoveries, scientific errors and also long hard work to get to the right product or scientific knowledge at the end.

Essay analysis

Paragraph 1

Many scientific errors and accidental discoveries have led to a greater attainment of scientific knowledge. There have been countless accidental discoveries, from normal everyday objects like Coke, Post-its and plastic, to everyday essentials like saccharin and smart dust (which monitors the water filtering system), and to medicinal discoveries such as penicillin, Viagra and the pacemaker. I will be looking at some famous examples of accidental discoveries, including penicillin, the pacemaker and radioactivity.

I like the structure of your introduction, although I think you can streamline it a little, eg there is some redundancy in repeating 'accidental discoveries'. I might have just removed your initial sentence and said 'There have been countless accidental discoveries leading to attainment of scientific knowledge, such as…'.

I like the way you've started with more random and esoteric examples, and then go on to focus on more medical examples – it's good to show the breadth of your knowledge, and also that you have a focus on and interest in medical examples. Good choices to use, which we will come on to.

Paragraph 2

Penicillin has been one of the most widely used antibiotics ever since Sir Alexander Fleming discovered it in 1928. He went away on holiday and forgot to clear his agar plates, and when he came back he observed that the colonies of the bacterium *Staphylococcus aureua* could be destroyed by the mould *Penicillium notatum* that grows naturally on fruit, proving that there was an antibacterial agent there. However, afterwards, Fleming couldn't culture penicillin and the project was abandoned until the 1940s during the Second World War, when Howard Florey and Ernst Chain isolated the active ingredient and developed an antibiotic that was used to help soldiers who had bacterial infections from their injuries in the war.

In essays, it is a good strategy to cover what you consider to be the key points first and then go on to distinguish yourself using outside-the-box techniques and examples – and you've done it well here. Penicillin is the classic example and I think you've executed it well, and with nice additional detail of the follow-up research. Beware of run-on sentences – consider a break at '… forgot to clean his agar plates. When he came back…'.

Paragraphs 3 and 4

The pacemaker came about when an American engineer called Wilson Greatbatch was working on a circuit that could help record fast heart sounds. He reached into the box for the resistor to complete the circuit and pulled out the wrong circuit part. Then the circuit pulsed in the same beat as the human heartbeat. Later, this was developed into a portable pacemaker that could be implanted into the human body and later actually into the heart.

Radioactivity was unknown until an accidental discovery when Henri Becquerel was using natural fluorescent minerals to study the properties of X-rays. When he exposed them to sunlight and then placed them on photographic plates wrapped in black paper, with a key on top, there was later a strong and clear image of the key on the photographic plates. He tested the effect further with the famous image of his wife's hand with her wedding ring.

I've grouped these paragraphs together because I think you are exhibiting a key technique here: the so-called 'packaged example'. This is an example which can be discussed from start to finish, with good and interesting detail, in two or three sentences. It is useful to have plenty of these in mind for both BMAT exams and Oxbridge interviews. They can underline key points and demonstrate your knowledge base in an economical and efficient manner. The pacemaker is a good example, but I think the radioactivity one is better. Remember that essays can become quite boring and monotonous at times for markers (interview answers also) and including interesting or amusing elements, such as the hand X-ray with the wedding ring, makes you stand out and will wake up the examiner.

Paragraphs 5 and 6

However, accidental discoveries and scientific errors do not always end up making amazing drugs or products. Most things need to be tested thoroughly and examined and rechecked before allowing that knowledge to be made fact. For example, many people thought that thalidomide was a fantastic discovery and helped to get rid of morning sickness in pregnant women. But a few months later, when the babies of mothers who had taken thalidomide were born deformed, researchers realized that they hadn't tested the drug on pregnant animals. Nowadays, having banned the drug from the stores, the pharmaceutical companies are researching the other effects of thalidomide on diseases and have found it to have an effect on leprosy.

A drug that was discovered accidentally is LSD, which was discovered in 1943 when Swiss chemist Albert Hofmann touched a chemical he was researching to induce childbirth and experienced the first acid hit. Since then, LSD has been used as a recreational drug, although it is harmful to the users and has been known to kill hundreds of users per year.

This is a great addition to your essay. It is important to see the opposite side of a question in answering essays, as this will give examiners the impression of a rounded and balanced argument. It also shows that you have insight to think outside the box. In this case, you have argued well that the statement is true, and used good and relevant examples. You have also said that errors do not always affect scientific knowledge in a positive way. This is a good point, but I think if I'm to be very strict, the fact that the results are sometimes bad does not necessarily stop them from affecting our scientific knowledge – in fact, thalidomide (good use of the example, by the way, and well explained succinctly) showed us, rather tragically, the effect of some drugs on fetuses. (Drugs that cause malformations are know as teratogens.) However, this is a well-made point.

I like the fact that you've used names and dates here; it sounds accomplished, and the history of science and medicine still has an important role in our knowledge today. Finally, Oxbridge tutors do love students who know a few of these things. I like the LSD example – though you should be careful in using casual language, eg 'acid hit' – this is street slang.

Paragraph 7

In conclusion, I think that scientific attainment has been effected to a great extent by scientific errors – even unsuccessful errors, as scientists have then gone back and checked over what had gone wrong and how it could be readjusted to make it right. The big scientific discoveries have been found through accidental discoveries, scientific errors and also long hard work to get to the right product or scientific knowledge at the end.

You have concluded very well, including the thought that scientific knowledge has also been influenced by research, experimentation and non-accidental application of data, for example in the jet engine, microprocessors and designer drugs targeting proteases in HIV and intracellular enzymes in cells. This shows that both errors and non-errors are involved in the attainment of scientific knowledge. Feel free to slip in an example or two casually here just to balance it with the weight of the rest of your essay – but a really nicely worked vision of both sides of the argument.

The other concept I want to introduce to you is quantitative linguistics. In this case, the quantitative statement made is 'to a great extent'. This would indicate that the contribution of errors has been large, perhaps more than 50 per cent. I might have used the above examples, coupled with your own, and said that scientific knowledge has certainly benefited from both errors and accurate research and application, and the above statement may be slightly generous to the role of errors and may neglect slightly the important of non-accidental discoveries.

Overall, good work, which demonstrates a solid breadth of knowledge, a pleasant writing style and organized structure. Stylistic things we can look to improve include removing redundancies in statements and avoiding colloquialism (be careful of terms like 'Coke' – use 'Coca-Cola'. Perhaps steer clear of Post-its, as this isn't very profound in terms of scientific discovery (secretaries might disagree with me, however); and 'acid hit' might be replaced with 'hallucinations'. In terms of Oxbridge applications, looking at both sides of the argument and appreciating quantitative linguistics are two key points to take home.

ADDITIONAL SAMPLE BMAT ESSAY 2

Describe the physiological differences in the body when rowing and sitting.

Human physiology is the biological study of the functions of living organisms and their various parts, and there are many organ systems that are affected by rowing and sitting, so I will concentrate on examining the main differences in the musculoskeletal system, the cardiovascular system and the endocrine system.

The musculoskeletal system is made up of the bones and muscles. There are three distinct types of muscles: skeletal muscles, cardiac muscles and smooth muscles. During rowing, the skeletal muscles will perform a coordinated contraction, moving the joints between the bones and permitting the person to move the legs and arms. While sitting, the skeletal muscles will be doing work, in a fixed contracted state allowing stability for the spine to support the torso, head and limbs. The cardiac muscle will be affected, as while the person is rowing, the heart muscle will be pumping harder and faster to allow the blood to flow more quickly around the body to supply more oxygen to the skeletal muscles to contract faster and harder and burn off any lactic acid produced. At the same time, carbon dioxide produced during cell respiration will be removed. However, when sitting, the cardiac muscle will be at the basal metabolic rate as there will be no voluntary movement apart from breathing and other essential activities, so the cardiac muscle will be beating at a slower rate. The smooth muscles are controlled by the autonomic nervous system and are involuntary. During rowing, as the heart rate is increased and more work is done, the person is getting hotter from the exercise. Owing to homeostasis, the capillaries, veins and arteries will undergo vasodilation near the surface of the skin to lose heat via radiation. When sitting, the smooth muscles will not undergo major change as there is no physical stress that is happening to the person.

The cardiovascular system consists of the heart and all the circulatory vessels. The main function is to distribute essential substances such as oxygen from the lungs to the cells and transport waste products from cell respiration such as carbon dioxide back to the lungs. The cardiovascular system also helps maintain homeostasis by stabilizing body temperature, blood pressure and pH of the blood. During strenuous physical exercise such as rowing, the heart beats at a much faster rate as the myogenic muscle is triggered to contract more quickly by the increased demand of oxygen and glucose for the increased rate of cell respiration. This also has an indirect effect on the body temperature as the rate of cell respiration has increased, so more heat is produced as a by-product, and the pores of the skin will open, sweat will be produced, the hairs on the skin will flatten and the blood vessels near the surface of the skin will dilate to radiate off the heat. The blood pressure will also increase, as the blood is flowing through the arteries at a much higher speed and the pH of the blood may also increase, if there is a build-up of lactic acid, if the muscle had to undergo anaerobic respiration if the blood did not supply the oxygen quickly enough. While sitting, the heart is at the BMR (basal metabolic rate), so the heart rate (between 60 and 100), blood pressure (around 120/80) and pH (around 7.4) will be normal.

The endocrine system is made up of ductless glands that produce hormones, which are an information signal system. During rowing, a hormone called adrenaline is produced and this acts on nearly all body tissues as it increases heart rate, respiratory rate, stimulates vasoconstriction or vasodilation and muscle contraction, all of which are essential for rowing. When sitting, there would be no hormones produced to act on the body at that one time, but other hormones may be around for a long-term effect, for example during puberty when there may be an increased amount of oestrogen or testosterone.

Essay analysis

Paragraph 1

Human physiology is the biological study of the functions of living organisms and their various parts, and there are many organ systems that are affected by rowing and sitting, so I will concentrate on examining the main differences in the musculoskeletal system, the cardiovascular system and the endocrine system.

I like your introduction in its overall structure. You have given a good definition of physiology. In terms of presentation, try to avoid run-on sentences that involve a linking all of the points you have made into one sentence going over several 'ands' and commas. You could, for example, make a natural break as follows: '… and their various parts. There are many…'. Making your sentences work with more punchy points will offer more clarity and help examiners to pause to digest each point in turn.

You could also streamline some phrasing such as 'I will concentrate on examining the main differences'. This could condense to 'I will focus on the main differences', which will make your writing more compact. This will be useful under time or word-limit pressures. I like the fact that you are using 'main differences', though – it will avoid you being criticized for leaving out small details, as you are focusing on the big topics.

Overall this is a good structure for the introduction; mainly there are some stylistic points to pick up on.

Paragraph 2

The musculoskeletal system is made up of the bones and muscles. There are three distinct types of muscles: skeletal muscles, cardiac muscles and smooth muscles. During rowing, the skeletal muscles will perform a coordinated contraction, moving the joints between the bones and permitting the person to move the legs and arms. While sitting, the skeletal muscles will be doing work, in a fixed contracted state allowing stability for the spine to support the torso, head and limbs. The cardiac muscle will be affected, as while the person is rowing, the heart muscle will be pumping harder and faster to allow the blood to flow more quickly around the body to supply more oxygen to the skeletal muscles to contract faster and harder and burn off any lactic acid produced. At the same time, carbon dioxide produced during cell respiration will be removed.

However, when sitting, the cardiac muscle will be at the basal metabolic rate as there will be no voluntary movement apart from breathing and other essential activities, so the cardiac muscle will be beating at a slower rate. The smooth muscles are controlled by the autonomic nervous system and are involuntary. During rowing, as the heart rate is increased and more work is done, the person is getting hotter from the exercise. Owing to homeostasis, the capillaries, veins and arteries will undergo vasodilation near the surface of the skin to lose heat via radiation. When sitting, the smooth muscles will not undergo major change as there is no physical stress that is happening to the person.

Again a good start. It is useful to stratify your answer by categories and discuss each one in turn. I like your selection of muscle types to do this. However, you have mixed the systems up a little: although bones and skeletal muscle are in the musculoskeletal system, cardiac muscle is more in the cardiovascular system, and smooth muscle in the digestive system for the most part. Also don't forget the accessory elements such as tendons and ligaments in the musculoskeletal system.

The main discussion of this essay is the differences in physiology, and you've come on to this well. In your discussion, I might have chosen to start with sitting rather than rowing, as this shows many of the basic functions of physiology, which then change, often increasing in a quantitative way, with rowing. However, your method is still valid, but it can flow more easily the other way around.

Good points made in this section. The main issue I have is that you have split the cardiovascular discussion between this paragraph and the one below. The discussion of CO_2 and O_2 could have been kept more to the cardiovascular system below, but fits in OK as you are discussing cardiac muscle. You've included smooth muscle detail, which is correct, but as in this case there is no difference between sitting and rowing, you could avoid these as you could be accused of not answering the question with that point.

Paragraph 3

The cardiovascular system consists of the heart and all the circulatory vessels. The main function is to distribute essential substances such as oxygen from the lungs to the cells and transport waste products from cell respiration such as carbon dioxide back to the lungs. The cardiovascular system also helps maintain homeostasis by stabilizing body temperature, blood pressure and pH of the blood. During strenuous physical exercise such as rowing, the heart beats at a much faster rate as the myogenic muscle is triggered to contract more quickly by the increased demand of oxygen and glucose for the increased rate of cell respiration. This also has an indirect effect on the body temperature as the rate of cell respiration has increased, so more heat is produced as a by-product, and the pores of the skin will open, sweat will be produced, the hairs on the skin will flatten and the blood vessels near the surface of the skin will dilate to radiate off the heat. The blood pressure will also increase, as the blood is flowing through the arteries at a much higher speed and the pH of the blood may also increase, if there is a build-up of lactic acid, if the muscle had to undergo anaerobic respiration if the blood did not supply the oxygen quickly enough. While sitting, the heart is at the BMR (basal metabolic rate), so the heart rate (between 60 and 100), blood pressure (around 120/80) and pH (around 7.4) will be normal.

Again, this is well done and I feel this paragraph is particularly thorough in its detail, which I like. Inclusion of temperature effects is good, and it's nice to see some quantitative information (although I would use the words 'average' or 'approximately' rather than 'around' as they sound more measured and scientific). The discussion of anaerobic or aerobic respiration is important and well done.

Paragraph 4

The endocrine system is made up of ductless glands that produce hormones, which are an information signal system. During rowing, a hormone called adrenaline is produced and this acts on nearly all body tissues as it increases heart rate, respiratory rate, stimulates vasoconstriction or vasodilation and muscle contraction, all of which are essential for rowing. When sitting, there would be no hormones produced to act on the body at that one time, but other hormones may be around for a long-term effect, for example during puberty when there may be an increased amount of oestrogen or testosterone.

The choice of endocrine systems is a good one, and I think you've covered the key point, which is adrenaline and its effects. It is important to consider that vasodilation occurs mainly in the skeletal muscle, as rate of flow of blood is dependent on the length of a vessel, but has a square relationship to the diameter of the vessel. This is an example of how to include knowledge from other scientific disciplines into medical essays, which is highly sought after, especially at Oxbridge. Again, with this paragraph try to avoid including things which do not demonstrate differences between sitting and rowing, such as oestrogen. For your reference, in the long-term training of rowers, athletes undergoing training will excrete more testosterone, which is a trophic agent for muscle (stimulates growth), as well as a growth hormone, and which comes from the pituitary gland.

Overall this is a good essay, with a clear structure and solid content. I have already commented on the issues with splitting the cardiovascular elements, which I think is the main downside of this essay. I felt that paragraph 2 was particularly strong and this reflects a good base of broad and deep scientific understanding. Other systems you could have touched on include the nervous system with discussion of nerves, action potentials and synapses involved in stimulating muscle contraction, as well as the respiratory system with effects such as changing the respiration rate and tidal volume of the lungs.

You could also discuss long-term effects such as increased lung capacity, muscle development, capillarization muscle and effects on joints (wear and tear leading to a risk of arthritis later on). It is impossible to cover everything, so I think you've had a good range; now think about your structure and phrasing where you can gain some extra marks.

Medical schools contacts list

Aberdeen

School of Medicine and Dentistry
3rd Floor, Polwarth Building
Foresterhill
Aberdeen
AB25 2ZD
Medical Admissions
Tel: +44 (0) 1224 554975
Fax: +44 (0) 1224 559978
E-mail: medadm@abdn.ac.uk
http://www.abdn.ac.uk/medicine-dentistry/

Belfast

School of Medicine, Dentistry and Biomedical Sciences
Health Sciences Building
97 Lisburn Road
Belfast
BT9 7BL
Tel: +44 (0) 2890 972349
Fax: +44 (0) 2890 972124
E-mail: pjmedschool@qub.ac.uk
http://www.qub.ac.uk/schools/SchoolofMedicineandDentistry

Birmingham

College of Medical and Dental Sciences
University of Birmingham
Edgbaston
Birmingham
B15 2TT
Tel: +44 (0) 121 414 3858
E-mail: mdsenquiries@contacts.bham.ac.uk
http://medweb.bham.ac.uk

Brighton Sussex

Brighton and Sussex Medical School
BSMS Teaching Building
University of Sussex
Brighton
East Sussex
BN1 9PX
Tel: +44 (0) 1273 643528/643529/641966
E-mail: medadmissions@bsms.ac.uk
http://www.bsms.ac.uk

Bristol

Faculty of Medicine and Dentistry
69 St Michael's Hill
Bristol
BS2 8DZ
Medical Admissions Assistant
Tel: +44 (0) 117 928 7679
E-mail: med-admissions@bristol.ac.uk
http://www.medici.bris.ac.uk

Cambridge

University of Cambridge School of Clinical Medicine
Addenbrooke's Hospital
Box 111
Hills Road
Cambridge
CB2 0SP
Tel: +44 (0) 1223 336700
Fax: +44 (0) 1223 336709
E-mail: admissions@medschl.cam.ac.uk
http://www.medschl.cam.ac.uk

Cardiff

Cardiff University School of Medicine
UHW Main Building
Heath Park

Cardiff
CF14 4XN
Tel: +44 (0) 29 2074 2020, ext 2020
Fax: +44 (0) 29 2074 3199
E-mail: meddean@cf.ac.uk
http://medicine.cf.ac.uk/

Dundee

School of Medicine
Dundee University
Perth Road
Dundee
Angus
DD1 4HN
Tel: +44 (0) 1382 632640
Fax: +44 (0) 1382 496391
E-mail: w.m.williamson@dundee.ac.uk
http://www.dundee.ac.uk/medicalschool

Durham

Durham University
School of Medicine and Health
Queen's Campus
University Boulevard
Stockton-on-Tees
TS17 6BH
Tel: +44 (0) 191 33 40353
E-mail: medicine.admissions@durham.ac.uk
http://www.dur.ac.uk/school.health/phase1.medicine

East Anglia

University of East Anglia
Norwich
NR4 7TJ
Tel: +44 (0) 1603 591515
E-mail: admissions@uea.ac.uk
http://www1.uea.ac.uk/cm/home/schools/foh/med

Edinburgh

College of Medicine and Veterinary Sciences
The University of Edinburgh
The Queen's Medical Research Institute
47 Little France Crescent
Edinburgh
EH16 4TJ
Tel: +44 (0) 131 242 9300
Fax: +44 (0) 131 242 9301
E-mail: mvm@ed.ac.uk
http://www.ed.ac.uk/schools-departments/medicine-vet-medicine

Glasgow

Medical School Office
University of Glasgow
Glasgow
G12 8QQ
Tel: +44 (0) 141 330 6216
Fax: +44 (0) 141 330 2776
E-mail: admissions@clinmed.gla.ac.uk
http://www.gla.ac.uk/faculties/medicine

Hull York

John Hughlings Jackson Building
University of York
Heslington
York
YO10 5DD
Tel: 0870 124 5500
Fax: +44 (0) 1904 321696
or
Hertford Building
University of Hull
Hull
HU6 7RX
Tel: 0870 124 5500
Fax: +44 (0) 1482 464705
http://www.hyms.ac.uk/

Keele

Keele University Medical School
City General Hospital
Newcastle Road
Stoke-on-Trent
Staffordshire
ST4 6QG
Tel: +44 (0) 1782 556556
Fax: +44 (0) 1782 556500
http://www.keele.ac.uk/health/schoolofmedicine/

Leeds

Leeds Institute of Medical Education
Room 7.09, Worsley Building
University of Leeds
Leeds
LS2 9JT
Tel: +44 (0) 113 343 7234
Fax: +44 (0) 113 343 4375
E-mail: A.E.Gaunt@leeds.ac.uk
http://www.leeds.ac.uk/medicine

Leicester

University of Leicester Medical School
Maurice Shock Building
PO Box 138
University Road
Leicester
LE1 9HN
Tel: +44 (0) 116 252 2969/2985/2966
Fax: +44 (0) 116 252 3013
E-mail: med-admis@le.ac.uk
http://www.le.ac.uk/sm/le

Liverpool

University of Liverpool
Liverpool
L69 3BX
Tel: +44 (0) 151 794 2000
E-mail: mbchb@liv.ac.uk
http://www.liv.ac.uk/medicine

Barts and The London School of Medicine and Dentistry

Barts and The London School of Medicine and Dentistry
Queen Mary, University of London
Garrod Building
Turner Street
Whitechapel
London
E1 2AD
Tel: +44 (0) 20 7882 8478/2243
E-mail: medicaladmissions@qmul.ac.uk
http://www.smd.qmul.ac.uk

King's College London

King's College London School of Medicine
First Floor, Hodgkin Building
Guy's Campus
London
SE1 1UL
Tel: +44 (0) 20 7848 6501
E-mail: ug-healthadmissions@kcl.ac.uk
http://www.kcl.ac.uk/schools/medicine

Imperial College London

Imperial College London
South Kensington Campus
London
SW7 2AZ
Tel: +44 (0) 20 7594 8056
E-mail: medicine.ug.admissions@imperial.ac.uk
http://www1.imperial.ac.uk/medicine

St George's London

St George's, University of London
Cranmer Terrace
London
SW17 0RE
Tel: +44 (0) 20 8672 9944
http://www.sgul.ac.uk

University College London

Medical Admissions Office
UCL Medical School
UCL
Gower Street
London
WC1E 6BT
Tel: +44 (0) 20 7679 0841
Fax: +44 (0) 20 7679 0890
E-mail: medicaladmissions@ucl.ac.uk
http://www.ucl.ac.uk/medicalschool/index.shtml

Manchester

School of Medicine
The University of Manchester
Oxford Road
Manchester
M13 9PT
Tel: +44 (0) 161 275 5025/5774
E-mail: ug.medicine@manchester.ac.uk
http://www.medicine.manchester.ac.uk

Newcastle

The Medical School
Newcastle University
Framlington Place
Newcastle upon Tyne
NE2 4HH
Tel: +44 (0) 191 222 5594
E-mail: enquiries@ncl.ac.uk
http://medical.faculty.ncl.ac.uk

Nottingham

University of Nottingham
Medical School
Queen's Medical Centre
Nottingham
NG7 2UH
Tel: +44 (0) 115 823 0000
Fax: +44 (0) 115 823 0004
E-mail: medschool@nottingham.ac.uk
http://www.nottingham.ac.uk/mhs

Oxford

Medical Sciences Office
John Radcliffe Hospital
Headington
Oxford
OX3 9DU
Tel: +44 (0) 1865 220313
E-mail: admissions@medschool.ox.ac.uk
http://www.medsci.ox.ac.uk

Peninsula

Peninsula College of Medicine and Dentistry
John Bull Building
Plymouth
PL6 8BU
Tel: +44 (0) 1752 437444
Fax: +44 (0) 1752 517842
E-mail: ku.ca.dmcp@ofni
http://www.pms.ac.uk/pms

Sheffield

The Medical School
University of Sheffield
Beech Hill Road
Sheffield
S10 2RX
Tel: +44 (0) 114 271 3349
Fax: +44 (0) 114 271 3960
E-mail: med-school@sheffield.ac.uk
http://www.shef.ac.uk/medicine

Southampton

Southampton General Hospital
Tremona Road
Southampton
Hampshire
SO16 6YD
Tel: +44 (0) 2380 594408
Fax: +44 (0) 2380 794760
E-mail: bmadmissions@soton.ac.uk
http://www.som.soton.ac.uk

St Andrews

Medical Admissions Officer
University of St Andrews
Admissions Application Centre
St Katherine's West
The Scores
St Andrews
Fife
KY16 9AX
Tel: +44 (0) 1334 462150
Fax: +44 (0) 1334 463330
http://medicine.st-andrews.ac.uk/prospectus/index.aspx

Swansea

School of Medicine
Swansea University
Singleton Park
Swansea
SA2 8PP
Tel: +44 (0) 1792 602618
Fax: +44 (0) 1792 602280
E-mail: medicine@swansea.ac.uk
http://www.swansea.ac.uk/medicine

Warwick

Warwick Medical School
University of Warwick
Coventry
CV4 7AL
Tel: +44 (0) 24 7652 4585
E-mail: wmsinfo@warwick.ac.uk
http://www2.warwick.ac.uk/fac/med/